HOWZZAT?

50 PREDICTIONS ON INDIAN CRICKET YOU WON'T BELIEVE!

GREENSTONE LOBO

Readomania

Readomania Publishing
A division of Kurious Kind Media Private Limited
466, DDA SFS Apartments, Pocket 1, Sector 22, Dwarka,
New Delhi – 110077
books.readomania.com
email: support@readomania.com
Facebook: facebook.com/iamreadomania
Twitter: twitter.com/iamreadomania

First Published in 2019 by Readomania

ISBN: 978-93-858543-2-3

Typeset in Palatino Linotype by Shine Graphics

Printed and bound at Thomson Press India Ltd.

Readomania

India has traditionally been the land of storytellers and a lot of us have an inherent skill of creating good plots, good stories and good narrations. With a little encouragement and support, many more authors will be widely read and attain a place in the sun. This is the essence of *Readomania*—an initiative that nurtures emerging stars of the literary world.

It would not be an exaggeration to say that *Readomania* is the talent hunt in fiction. It goes a step beyond by not just identifying the talent but also nurturing it and showcasing it to the world. In the process, we have created a powerhouse of content.

Readomania has four principal interest areas—traditional print publishing, online library of short stories and poetry, literary events and products.

The print publishing works towards delivering good quality content to the readers. We publish good authors in meaningful anthologies, novels and works of narrative non-fiction. Our books stand out for their perspectives, the plots, the language and most importantly their ability to enrich lives.

Take a break, read something nice, write something beautiful. Read our books or visit us at www.readomania.com and enjoy a whole new world of literature.

Dedicated to all the sportspersons of India, especially the cricketers who obliged me with their complete and accurate birth details. The data helped me immensely in my research. It also enabled me to help others who are either already pursuing or want to pursue various sports.

Contents

1

Introduction

Sherlock Holmes with his fancy hat, magnifying glass and pipe always fascinated me. I was glued to every clue Perry Mason worked on. I would read with anticipation as Ganesh (Vasanth) reconstructed a crime with a seemingly simple object. The way these celebrated detectives worked was really captivating—piecing clues together, painstakingly, one piece at a time, sometimes aided by past theories and sometimes devising new techniques to help in the search.

Probably, it is a thing with all Scorpios. They love the mysteries of the world. So do I. And I have a snoopy Aquarian in me too, who also loves hidden somethings and suspense. At the age when most boys' fantasies involved picking up a bat and destroying the opposition to win a cricket match for their country, I would fantasise myself as a detective solving a murder mystery with a simple clue.

While that dream of being a detective never materialised, I'm truly grateful to the universe's way of giving me a chance to be a detective in my own way. Only, there is no violent death that I investigate; it is life—the past, the present and, most importantly, the future, for that's where one's hopes and aspirations lie. And yes, I don't have a Dr Watson or a Vasanth to talk to. It's myself that I engage with. If people in my inner circle feel that I'm lost most of the time, then they are right. And some of them also know it is the normal state for me.

This is a slice of my life story—the story of how I go about making my predictions. On different occasions, if I refer to a past prediction of mine, it is only to help you marvel at the amazing accuracy of astrology. My aim is to explain, in simple words, that astrology is more science than art. It is something that can be learnt and taught. In fact, replicated too.

In this book, I will show you the power of astrology through a study—a study of the game of gentlemen. We are talking about cricket and certain important events connected with it. The men mentioned here were destined for greatness and achieved it. But they too cannot achieve more than what is destined. And, yes, you cannot only measure their success quotient, but also predict when life will cease to be magical for them. All of this can be predicted just by looking at the positions of the planets over the horizon when the person was born.

Sports outcomes are some of the most unpredictable things in the world. Investment banks like Commerzbank, UBS and Goldman Sachs tried to predict the 2018 Football World Cup, by simulating factors and conditions used in predicting financial market movements.

Well, all the three banks couldn't get it right[1].

---

[1] Kelleher, K. (2018, June 27). *UBS, Commerzbank models predicted Germany would win the world cup. Why predicting sports is bad business.* Retrieved from: http://fortune.com. Accessed on 17 February 2019.

In this book, I'm going to show you how, by just using a handful of variables, the outcome of even such a supposedly 'unpredictable' event can be predicted. We will see how the biggest spectacle of 'the game of glorious uncertainties' can be a 'certain' event.

Contrary to popular belief, astrology is more about logic and less about numbers. The various events and thought processes that led to certain assumptions have been mentioned in the first few chapters. Then the 50 predictions follow. If you are short of time and patience, you can jump directly to the predictions. If you are someone who likes to know how particular conclusions were derived/arrived at, then the chapters leading to the actual predictions would probably interest you.

I will also introduce you to the techniques that aid me and new ideas I have formulated. I also aim to make you see and admire the science in astrology. This book is not aimed at making you an astrologer though. So, I have reserved all the complicated theories and terminologies for a future book dedicated to that.

This book will also show that we are all bound by our karmas. One cannot reap what he hasn't sown. One cannot achieve more in life than is destined. But, if you are destined for greatness, no one can stop you either. In short, your destiny is pre-written. And one cannot change one's destiny.

2

Kapil's Devils, Ranatunga's Asuras and the Planet Pluto

25th June 1983. Tuticorin.

Cricket zoomed into my life when I was eleven. Growing up in the southernmost part of India, until then my heroes had been Kamal Haasan, Ilaiyaraaja and SP Balasubrahmanyam. The only footballer I knew was Pele and never knew sports like cricket and tennis existed. Suddenly, everything changed. India won its first cricket World Cup in 1983 and everyone was talking about Kapil Dev and the game that had established India's stardom across the world—the game that would eventually become a religion for this nation.

Though cricket was introduced by the British in the 1700s, and India became a test-playing nation in 1932, it was probably this landmark victory that made it a superpower in the sport. The introduction of television only revolutionised it. Cricket had entered into India's everyday life, slowly and surely. I sat up and took notice too. And, yes, I had a new set of heroes to look up to.

The way this game touches people has always fascinated me. People will not move from a particular chair when a match is on; some will wear their lucky shirt to make their team win, and some will not shave during the whole cricket season. Cricket has the power to make even the strongest of atheists believe in superstitions, at least in India.

My father worked in the Bombay docks (yes, it was Bombay then) and I used to visit him sometimes. We were a large family. I was the eldest with five younger brothers and a sister. As education in Mumbai wasn't affordable, Mom shifted with the kids to our native place in Tamil Nadu. During one of my visits to Bombay, on a rainy day in 1986, I picked up Linda Goodman's *Sun Signs* from the sidewalks of the Churchgate station. It will sound clichéd if I say my life changed forever but, believe me, it did! My fascination for astrology grew after I reached my small hometown. I started collecting and reading as many works on astrology as I could lay my hands upon. The librarian opposite my school was surprised to see a fourteen year old's interest changing from detective novels to astrology books almost overnight.

In 1989, I came to Mumbai to do my graduation. I had always been in love with the city. My fascination for this huge megalopolis only grew. During lonely hours at Marine Drive, where I sat and watched gigantic waves of the Arabian Sea strike the huge concrete tetrapods standing in an interlocked pattern on the shore, I would often wonder what I would be doing in my life twenty years later.

I wanted to provide whatever financial support I could to my family at the earliest. I completed my graduation from Mumbai University in the mid-90s and immediately took up a job as a salesperson with a multinational company, which posted me in the far-off Jabalpur. Thus, in my early twenties, I was working in the largest state in India. Madhya Pradesh hadn't parted ways with Chattisgarh then. Sometimes, just the travel time from one city to another was a couple of days. With plenty of time on hand, I found myself drifting towards researching various phenomena in astrology, which was fast turning into a passion. I had numerous astrology books for company.

My intention was very simple: I wanted to know what I would end up doing in my life. Once I learnt how to, I read the charts of hundreds of famous people to see if there were any planetary clues that could show what *my* career would eventually turn out to be. Besides this, I wanted to know what made someone a filmstar, a musician or a politician. I was also keen to know how sportstars created such a huge impact within a short span in their career.

Somewhere during those long travels on work, I had a brainwave. I wondered if astrology could help predict the results of events like a World Cup. The euphoria and the pride that surrounded that historic victory by Kapil's Devils made me look at cricket once again, this time from the perspective of astrology.

In those times, when there was no Google or other websites, the only source of birth data were the astrology books. It was during the 1996 World Cup that I really made a serious effort to predict the outcome of a sports event. No, I didn't go and publish it in the papers, and not many would have published the prediction of a twenty-four-year-old learner. It was simply a personal validation of the possibility of using astrology to predict events.

I collated the data on the birth dates of all the cricket captains of the various countries participating in the 1996 World Cup. As it was not possible to find every player's birth details, I had to make do with the information available about the captains. What was initially a deterrent became a blessing in disguise later when I discovered that the captain's horoscope is the best indicator of the team's results.

I found that Arjuna Ranatunga, the captain of the Sri Lankan team, had the best horoscope amongst all the captains. Now, by 'best' I mean what I guessed to be outstanding amongst all others at that time, based on certain parameters I was aware of, and on my own limited understanding of astrology in those days. I didn't know then that there were still many things about the subject to be learned.

I found that Arjuna Ranatunga was born on a full-moon day, which is considered as auspicious. Besides, the burly Lankan captain also had Saturn in its own house, a very powerful planet, so his chances were brighter, I concluded. Interestingly, the Indian captain, Mohd Azharuddin, too, was born on a full-moon day, but Arjuna's day was better as the full moon was exalted too at that time. Well, that was *my* theory.

And, you know what? Sri Lanka actually won the World Cup!

I was elated.

Now, I had found my secret mantra for predicting sports events. This was going to be my favourite pastime from now on. But I didn't realise that even a stopped clock shows the correct time twice a day. The truth dawned upon me three years later in 1999.

Circa 1999

I saw an astrological marvel happening in the World Cup that year. When I collected the birth details of the captains, to my surprise, I found that almost each of them from the major cricketing nations was born on a full-moon day. India's Mohd Azharuddin, West Indies's Brian Lara (yes, West Indies was a major cricketing nation then), England's Alec Stewart, Pakistan's Wasim Akram, South Africa's Hansie Cronje, Sri Lanka's Arjuna Ranatunga—all were born on full-moon days, a pattern too obvious to dismiss as a coincidence for an astrologer. Well, even a minor cricketing nation Zimbabwe's Alistair Campbell was born on a full-moon day. Only Australia's Steve Waugh and New Zealand's Stephen Fleming were not born on full-moon days. I dismissed Australia as Steve Waugh didn't have a great horoscope anyway.

I thought some full-moon guy would win, probably Brian Lara. After all, he was born on the most powerful full-moon day. He was born with the sun in exaltation and the full moon in Libra. That was Buddha Poornima and it was supposed to be the most auspicious day of the year. He was probably the best bet as the World Cup winner. With the bowling line-up he had in his team, and his batting abilities well backed by some great batsmen, he was the most obvious choice. So, this was my prophecy and I waited to see how the events would unfold.

Unbelievably, for me, Steve Waugh's Australia won the World Cup after facing defeat and having been on the verge of elimination in the tournament. This was incredible not just for me from the astrological perspective but also from a purely cricketing perspective. There was a time when they had to win seven matches in a row to win the Cup, a feat which seemed nearly impossible, that is, until they actually did it. A team which was on the verge of elimination rose like the phoenix and won every consecutive match they played.

It was shocking. How had they done that? Steve Waugh's victory made me ecstatic. Of course, my failed prediction made me a little sad, but is there a better way to learn if not from your own failures? I thought there was something in it for me to take lessons from. There was something in Steve Waugh's horoscope I had missed, which had pushed him to win the World Cup. What was it? Had I overlooked something? How was I to know that I had omitted an entire *planet* in my analysis? I realised it over a period of time, after a great deal of research.

The new millennium had dawned by now and I had started using MS-Excel for my research work. The invention by the richest man in the world was making life easier for everyone, including me. The various analytics and matrices used in sales helped tabulate the birth data of the sports stars.

During one such tabulation I realised another thing: the emerging film superstars in those years, Shah Rukh Khan, Salman Khan and Aamir Khan, all three were born in the same year as Steve Waugh—1965. Something had certainly eluded the eye—the year 1965.

I had to move away from the way traditional Indian astrologers practised astrology and based their predictions on mundane events. Indian astrologers never looked beyond Saturn in their calculations. In a later book, I will talk about why this is a problem.

Here, let me just say that I started including planets like Uranus, Neptune and Pluto in my calculations. And voila, it worked!

Later, I discovered that the only common factor between Steve Waugh and the three Khans was the planet Pluto. All three of them had Pluto between 23 and 27 degrees in the zodiac sign Leo. This is the point of the deepest exaltation (the best celestial position) for this planet. This marvel happened once in about 260 years. Now, that was something! The Khans and Waugh had something really rare in them and hence could become superstars or win the World Cup.

We all are born different. Many may have exalted planets in their birth chart and achieve successes in their lives, but those with the planets in deepest exaltation achieve that rare distinction and become the biggest achievers. The deepest exaltation indicates the planet reaching a particular degree in a particular zodiac sign. For example, Neptune gets deeply exalted at 25 degrees in Cancer, Taurus, Libra and Sagittarius. There may be many with Neptune in exaltation in their charts, but Shah Rukh Khan is Shah Rukh Khan *because* he has the planet of illusion, Neptune, in *deepest* exaltation in his first house (of personality), which makes him a king in the world of showbiz. And isn't showbiz all about creating alluring illusions?

Steve Waugh's win also showed me that the planet Pluto had three exaltation points. The second exaltation point was present in Kapil Dev's birth chart—Kapil Dev, who won the first World Cup for India. The third exaltation point had won it for Steve Waugh and

Australia. Well, which was the first one? It happened in 1949–52. We will talk about that phenomenon a little later.

This was the beginning of my long and arduous journey into the mysteries of astrology. I thanked my stars that I had been wrong this time. If I hadn't been wrong, I wouldn't have learnt about Pluto. I had formulated some theories and decided to experiment with them during the next World Cup. Sometimes they worked, sometimes they didn't. But now I had started taking serious interest in cricket and its connection to my world of astrology. I followed every World Cup since then. I looked at the horoscopes of the players and speculated about the top team that would win the Cup.

I saw a change in myself where I no longer hated the Australians because they were on a winning spree. Instead, I was highly upset when I felt someone who deserved to be in the Indian team wasn't there, someone who could win us the World Cup.

Every time my prognosis went wrong, I learnt something new. Every time the Aussies won, I stumbled upon a new discovery. The entire phase from 1996 to 2007 was a huge learning curve for me, especially in sports astrology. I didn't realise then that all the mistakes I committed would lead to new learning and something even more interesting—something that would make me wonder about the fundamentals of astrology, especially the kind practised in India.

3

The Superstar Theory

2000–2010. Bhopal, Indore, Mumbai.

Arjuna Ranatunga and Steve Waugh's victories in 1996 and 1999 clearly established the power of the farthest planet in the solar system, Pluto, on the lives of human beings. The revelation of Pluto and the unfolding of the secrets during the years 1949–68 (when Pluto was in the zodiac sign Leo, its exaltation point) motivated me to do further research on the planet and its far-off cousins, Uranus, Neptune, *et al*, so that I didn't receive any new surprises connected with these distant bodies.

Though there are 12 zodiac signs, in Indian astrology we use only five planets—Mercury, Venus, Mars, Jupiter and Saturn—as their rulers. The sun and the moon are not supposed to be considered as planets here as they are luminaries or stars. The Western astrologers use four more bodies, namely Uranus, Neptune, Pluto and Chiron. That adds up to nine planets. As there are 12 houses in a zodiac wheel, it makes sense that there should be 12 planets ruling them. My research pointed to the existence of three missing bodies as those missing links. I needed to know about them since they would assure greater accuracy in theorising about the possibility of an event happening in the future, be it sports or anything else.

By the time I finished my research on Uranus, Neptune and Pluto and turned my attention to the other missing links in astrology, two more World Cups had passed—in 2003 and in 2007. I was clueless in both these World Cups about who would win them. I couldn't come to a proper conclusion since I didn't have any clinching astrological evidence to ascertain which captain would win the Cup for his country. All the captains were born in the early 70s and their charts didn't offer solid indications regarding the best planet placements. Or maybe I could not read the signs clearly enough.

Interestingly, Ricky Ponting, who won both these World Cups, had none of the traditional planets in strong positions. It was perplexing that he didn't even have Uranus, Neptune or Pluto in strong positions.

After intense research for over a decade, I found that there were three more planetoids (let me call them Planet-X, Planet-Y and Planet-Z), besides Chiron, which needed to be added to the analysis if I wanted to know who would win the next World Cup.

Planet-X is an unnamed centaur (akin to an asteroid) that lies between Saturn and Uranus. The astronomical code given by NASA to this body is 2007 RH283. Similarly, Planet-Y is also a centaur orbiting between Saturn and Uranus and the NASA number for it is 1999 JV127, while Planet-Z orbits in the same centaur belt and is numbered 2008 FC76. I call them Planet-X, Planet-Y and Planet-Z for the sake of convenience.

I consider these three bodies as the missing links in astrology that help me zero in on the future World Cup winners.

I was shocked to see that Ricky Ponting had these planets X, Y and Z in the best positions therefore, he could win World Cups back to back. The entire army of the Aussie cricketers, who played under him, had these three planets in strong positions.

I had all my questions answered now and understood why it was Ricky Ponting and not Sourav Ganguly who had won the battle in the finals of the 2003 World Cup.

So, who after Ricky Ponting?

I was extremely enthusiastic about the next superstar in cricket. I had to find this guy. Where was he born? Was it possible that he could be Indian? How nice it would be if this were true! I started searching diligently for the man who would be the next 'great' in cricket.

Ponting was born in 1974. Many other sports legends, too, were born around 1972–74. In fact many actors, singers and hugely successful celebrities even from other fields were born during these years. I looked for the next period after 1972–74 that would show a big spurt in the number of mega-achievers. Many indicators pointed at 1981–82 to be the next great astrological season.

Looking at the other sports, I picked up some clues regarding the year in which the next superstar of cricket would be born. After the early-1970s-born Andre Agassi and Pete Sampras (both American), it was the 1981-born Roger Federer (Swiss) who had become the undisputed superstar in tennis. Iker Casillas from Spain was making waves and had attained an iconic status in football with extraordinary successes after the 1973-born Fabio Cannavaro from Italy.

In women's tennis, it was a straight jump from the 1969-born Steffi Graf (German) to the 1981-born Serena Williams (American). After the Bollywood superstar

Hrithik Roshan—a 1974-born, Ranbir Kapoor and Shahid Kapoor were the rising superstars of Bollywood, born in 1981–82. There was something about this period of 1980–82, especially 1981. All pointers indicated that the next superstar in cricket had to be someone born in 1981.

It is interesting to note that great people come in clusters. I mean, all the greats of the world are born during similar/same moments in time. They may be great in different fields, but their grandeur would be similar.

We can extrapolate that from the birth year of superstars from other fields. Let me explain with a few examples.

Did you know that the famous superstars of the Indian film industry, Amitabh Bachchan, Jeetendra and Rajesh Khanna were born in the same year—1942? Now, besides the Bollywood legends, even Western legends—musicians like Paul McCartney, Barbara Streisand, Jimi Hendrix and also the Einstein of our generation, Stephen Hawking, were born in the same year. Also the greatest boxing champion ever, Mohammed Ali. The World Cup-winning Italian football legend and one of the greatest footballers of all time, Bobby Moore, Eusebio, and the greatest football manager in the history of the sport, Alex Ferguson, too, were born in 1941–42. The all-time leader in the history of the Grand Prix motorcycle racing, Giacomo Agostini, was another one born in 1942.

Planet-X was in deepest and greatest exaltation in 1941–42. As we can see, either legends, or at least the most powerful people from various fields, were born during this period. And if you think 1942 was an aberration, the next set was born in 1944–46. This was the time when Planet-X was deeply exalted and Planet-Y was in its own house, the zodiac sign Virgo. You can gauge the importance of this span by the simple fact that there were three American presidents born in 1946: George W. Bush, Bill Clinton and—guess who—even Donald Trump, with a total of five presidential terms between them! Big screen legends like Sylvester Stallone, Steven Spielberg and Michael Douglas were born in this period too. So were the football legend, Franz Beckenbauer and the basketball legend, Phil Jackson.

In cricket, Clive Lloyd, the first super-successful captain from West Indies, was born in 1944. He was the chosen one to win the first cricket World Cup. In fact, the two strongest planets in his horoscope—X and Y—gave him two World Cup wins—in 1975 and 1979.

The next important spell was 1950–52, where Pluto was in its positive exaltation. The men who had seen great adversities in life, or who were from humble backgrounds and had risen to script extraordinary stories, were born in this period. Prime Minister Narendra Modi was one. Apart from actor Rajinikanth, tennis legends Jimmy Connors, Guillermo Vilas; football legend Dino Zoff, the 1980 hockey gold-winning V Bhaskaran and Mark Spitz, the swimming legend, were some of the extraordinary sports heroes to be born in this duration. Cricket produced the legendary Imran Khan, who was born in 1952 and won the 1992 World Cup at the age of 40. Besides Pluto, Imran Khan also had Saturn in exaltation in his horoscope. Saturn indicates late success and hence Imran Khan achieved peak success at a later age.

The next great period was 1954–55. Saturn and Jupiter were in exaltation simultaneously during these years. This strong phenomenon happens once in about sixty years. While Indian actors Kamal Haasan and Chiranjeevi, Hong Kong actor Jackie Chan and American talk show host Oprah Winfrey are examples of screen legends, France's Michel Platini is the most famous football legend, and Chris Evert (American) is one of the best-known tennis greats. Great entrepreneurs like Bill Gates and Steve Jobs (American) were born in this stretch too. The cricket World Cup was won by the 1955-born legend, Allan Border, of Australia, in 1987.

Next came the negative exaltation of Pluto in the years 1958–61. The legends born in these years saw some extraordinary success, but also faced some troubled times in their lives: Argentina's football legend, Diego Maradona; Ayrton Senna—the legendary F1 champion from Brazil; John McEnroe—the American tennis champion and the American basketball champion, Magic Johnson.

History was made when India (outsiders with a 500:1 possibility of winning, according to the book makers) won the cricket World Cup for the first time in 1983, under the captaincy of the 1959-born Kapil Dev. Indian actor, Sanjay Dutt, and the American singers, Michael Jackson and Madonna, are legends personified—who had Pluto in negative exaltation in their charts. All these 1958–61-born legends had some tragic incidents in their lives. Even Barack Obama, a 1961-born, became the president when America was going through its worst economic crisis.

The next best period came in 1963–64. A positive Pluto was in exaltation and Saturn was also in a strong position. The people born then achieved success, yes, but after facing tough ordeals and many obstacles. Besides Sri Lanka's Arjuna Ranatunga, examples include Michael Jordan—the basketball legend from America. American actors, Brad Pitt and Johnny Depp; singer Whitney Houston, Indian actress Sridevi and Canadian actor, Keanu Reaves, are the legends from the field of entertainment born during this period.

The subsequent great planetary marvel happened in 1965–67. Pluto was in its deepest positive exaltation. People with this placement saw dizzying successes and became the undisputed numero uno in their trade, but they also faced some tragedies in their lives. It is interesting to note that the greatest superstars of our times—Shah Rukh Khan, Salman Khan and Aamir Khan, all were born in 1965. The only superstar not from the *'Khan'dan*—Akshay Kumar—was born in 1967. And so was the musical legend, AR Rahman.

The golden period after that was 1972–74, where Planet-X and Planet-Z moved into strong positions. We will discuss these planets in detail later. But I must tell you that the Fab Four of Indian cricket were born in this very period—Sourav Ganguly, Rahul Dravid, Sachin Tendulkar and VVS Laxman. So was Ricky Ponting, who won the World Cup in 2003 and 2007—one each for Planet-X and Planet-Z.

As you can see, every time there is a major planetary phenomenon, the best in the business are born. This can be applied to any industry. I conducted extensive research on this subject and noticed that even organisations born during a great planetary phenomenon can have a great future. For example, India's greatest wealth creator, Reliance, was established in 1966—the same period as the Khans. So, Reliance is the Shah Rukh Khan amongst industries. Microsoft established in early 1975 is the Hrithik Roshan or Ricky Ponting of the industry. Take a look at the next great wealth creator—Infosys—established on 2nd July 1981—the week when MS Dhoni was born!

Can this also be reverse engineered? YouTube, Google and Facebook were born in the 2000s. You can examine these years carefully and predict in which year the greatest future superstars will be born. Or look at any sports star's birth details and find out how far they will go in their career. I arrived at this simple theory after examining hundreds of horoscopes of sports stars, screen legends, entertainers and political figures.

Coming back to the 2011 World Cup, who would be the next superstar?

In the period between 2007 and 2010, this was the biggest question in my life. I looked in every direction and hung on to every clue possible to know who that would be. Interestingly, I got a clue about who would win the 2011 cricket World Cup while studying other sports like tennis, football and even shooting and the Olympics. And all pointers pointed in one direction: that superstar would be born in the year 1981.

Yes, the 1981 phenomenon was probably the greatest for a sportsperson born in the 21st century! We were very lucky that in cricket, that superstar was born in India!

4

Lessons from Football

7th July 2006. Mumbai.

I remember the date distinctly. It was India's brave young wicketkeeper Dhoni's 25th birthday and the newspapers had wished him well. On that Friday morning, I was waiting to meet the head of Talent Management of a multinational bank for the final round of a job interview for the position of a training manager.

Anupa Sadasivan looked too young to be in that position. However, I understood why she was there when she started asking those intelligent, probing questions for which not many would have been prepared. She brought out my characteristics clearly in her attempt to know if I was the right fit for the job advertised. One of her questions was, 'So, what do you do to de-stress?' I told her about astrology being my passion and how doing research on sports astrology was therapeutic for me. She was intrigued and probed further for examples. I explained how I had researched on cricket and how I thought a 1981-born would win a World Cup. I even said that Dhoni, whose birthday it was that day, could win a World Cup for India if he was made the captain.

Then I looked straight into her eyes and said with a theatrical effect, 'I'm going to predict something that will come true two days from now. On the 9th of July 2006, when Italy meets France in the football World Cup final, Italy will win.'

She was taken aback. Then she smiled and said, 'Consider your job confirmed if Italy wins.'

I smiled too.

Italy won. I received my offer letter and joined the bank. Even today I'm not sure if it was the astrological prediction that did the trick or my knowledge and experience in the domain of learning and development. A decade after that incident, Anupa who is now the HR country head of one of the largest banks in the world still wouldn't tell me. HR people have to keep certain secrets to themselves, you see.

Now, if you ask me how I deduced Italy winning the World Cup, well...it was very simple. The two captains in the final were the 1973-born Fabio Cannavaro (Italy) and the 1972-born Zinedine Zidane (France). This was almost like the India versus Australia Cricket World Cup final in 2003—Sourav Ganguly (1972-born) versus Ricky Ponting (1974-born). I saw that Zidane had a horoscope very similar to Ganguly's and Cannavaro's was closer to Ponting's. Planet-X and Planet-Z both were more powerful in Cannavaro's horoscope. I had used the cricket logic to arrive at a football prediction. Later on, during my research, I realised that vice-versa happened more often.

Though I always wished that I would be better known for my credentials as a facilitator, trainer and coach, this interview incident made me more popular for being a predictor of sports events. The next big event happened in 2007 and I predicted to my colleagues that India would not win the World Cup under Rahul Dravid, but also that I wasn't sure which team's captain would. Ricky Ponting, the 1974-born, had already won it in 2003. Now, the sequence of the birth year of the captains who had won the biggest prize in cricket looked like this—1944-1959-1955-1952-1963-1965-1974. The next year in the sequence, using astrology, had to be 1981. But I wasn't sure whether the 1972–74-patch had produced only one World Cup winner or more.

Looking at Dravid's horoscope I knew that there were many other captains who had equivalent or better horoscopes—such as England's Michael Vaughan or even New Zealand's Stephen Fleming. I was also wary of the threat posed by Brian Lara of West Indies and Inzamam-ul-Haq of Pakistan, who were born in 1969–70. The 1969–70 period was very important and hadn't produced a World Cup winner in cricket yet. In football, the previous World Cup winner had been the 1970-born Cafu. So, I wasn't sure. Besides, there was this young man, Graeme Smith, born in 1981, who captained South Africa (SA). Their team looked menacing too. If the sequence of the years went as I believed, then even SA could win this time. I thought I was going to learn a lot from that World Cup and decided not to hazard a prediction but to just wait and watch.

In 2008, I left my job at the bank to join an insurance company. This was to become the company where I would stay for over a decade—until the end of my corporate career, when I decided to focus solely on astrology.

When I resigned from the bank, the sales director, Vikas Agnihotri, a football fan, after wishing me good luck, winked and said, 'And keep sending me those football predictions.' Wow! It was heartening to know that people in high positions, too, were keen to know my views. Vikas was someone who didn't believe in barriers. Anyone could walk up to him at any time. And that reflected the culture of the bank. But it made me happy that I was noticed—if not directly for my profession, then at least for my passion.

That was the power of sports. I remember predicting that Spain would win the UEFA Euro in 2008. Vikas promised me a lunch treat if that indeed happened. He was busy then. Now, as the country head of one of the largest companies in the world, he is perhaps busier than ever. Vikas, you still owe me that lunch!

Euro 2008 gave me even more confidence to proceed with my research on cricket. I decided to continue with my explorations in the field of sports predictions. Wouldn't it be great if I could announce to the world who would win the next cricket World Cup in 2011? I thought it would just be a pipe dream, until it actually happened. But I had to thank football once again for that.

5

Dhoni and the Uranus Connection

23rd December 2004. Mumbai.

I was thrilled to find that the Fab Four of Indian cricket, Sachin Tendulkar, Sourav Ganguly, VVS Laxman and Rahul Dravid, were born in the patch 1972–74, the same patch I was born in. It was very important, personally, to know which planets ruled this period since those planets were the key to understanding my own career. By 2005 I knew that these were Planet-X and Planet-Z.

I discovered that one of these planets was in my ninth house. The ninth house of a horoscope indicates being a subject matter expert, a teacher, a writer or a coach. I was thrilled to find that those were precisely the areas where my interests lay. I had gradually shifted from sales to training after doing my Master's in Human Resources. I had relocated to Mumbai from Madhya Pradesh and was now working with the largest FMCG company in the country. Keen students of astrology would know that even astrology is ruled by the ninth house. I was super happy that I was headed in the right direction. I had been able to use the vocational guidance of astrology upon myself.

I found out that Planet-Z and Planet-X gave you success over a period of time. Rarely did they make you a phenomenon overnight. Consequently, I asked myself if there were planets which made someone a success overnight, just like that! I got my answer soon.

Sourav Ganguly had wondered[1] where MS Dhoni was when India was playing the 2003 World Cup final against Australia. Well, Dhoni was a ticket collector with the Indian Railways at that time. Sourav can be excused if he believes that had Dhoni played the finisher, he would have won the match against the mighty Aussies that year. But Sourav is not aware of the fact that Uranians don't progress steadily; they arrive suddenly and like a hurricane.

Now, let us talk about the planet which makes the man Mahendra Singh Dhoni—the planet which won him the first World Cup of the game in its newest avatar.

Uranus rules all inventions, discoveries and ground-breaking ideas. Isn't that cool? Yes, Uranus really is the cool dude of the zodiac. People associated with this planet are eccentric and non-conformist geniuses. Somehow I liked this strange planet with its electric-blue hues. As I have the moon in the Uranus-ruled Aquarius myself, I could understand the idiosyncrasies and eccentricities associated with them. But never did I imagine that my research would lead me to pinpoint its exact exaltation point—an original discovery.

---

1 Patra, S. (2018, March 01). *'Wish he was in my 2003 world cup team,' writes Sourav Ganguly.* Retrieved from https://sports.ndtv.com. Accessed on 17 February 2019.

Uranus was discovered in 1781 by the English astronomer, Sir William Herschel. It is a humongous planet, fourteen times the size of Earth and its movement has been described as erratic[2]. Uranus rotates on a whopping 98-degree tilt! Basically, its north and south poles are where the Earth's equator would be. However, the strangest thing about it is its erratic magnetosphere. A magnetosphere is the magnetism surrounding a planet. Unlike Earth and Jupiter's, which are pretty much constant, the magnetic field on Uranus turns on and off as if someone is flipping a switch.

This different orbit and magnetosphere is indicative of the rebelliously innovative views of its children. Its discovery also roughly coincided with the French and American revolutions. It is truly a planet that influences new thoughts and fosters mutinous views.

The influence of Uranus can bring in sudden but progressive changes in society. People with a strong Uranus never bend to rules; rather, they set their own principles and pace, and believe in the disruption of the old order. They are inventive, rebellious, original and resourceful. They have a strong need to be different from the herd though sometimes it can be rebellion for rebellion's sake, they can also be harbingers of change.

Uranus rules Aquarius. It also rules the brain, especially the pituitary gland. The symbol for Uranus is a cross atop a circle, flanked on each side by a half circle.

---

[2] Apex Magnets. (2017, June 30). *The erratic magnetism of Uranus.* Retrieved from: https://apexmagnets.com. Accessed on 17 February 2019.

It signifies a spirit ruled by its mind. It also signifies a synthesis of the attributes of all the planets.

Interestingly, Uranus is the ruling planet of our cricket superstar, Mahendra Singh Dhoni. It rules one half of him. The genius of Dhoni can be attributed to Uranus. His quicksilver brainwork that often left people dazed and was lauded as the master stroke of a genius—was simply the consequence of Uranus.

Dhoni has all the trappings of Uranus. The first four matches he played were insignificant as he came lower down the order. He burst on the scene suddenly in Visakhapatnam on 5th April 2005 with his match-winning knock against Pakistan when Ganguly decided to promote him to number three. He had never been noticed in the Under-16 or Under-19 matches. He had never played an Under-19 World Cup like Virat Kohli or Yuvraj Singh. Nor had he made hundreds of runs like VVS Laxman in the domestic circuit before being drafted into the Indian team.

Dhoni *looked* different. He had Greek-god looks with a lion-like mane. He won the inaugural T20 World Cup in South Africa in September 2007. T20 was the newest form of cricket at that time that was revolutionising the sport. When T20 was invented in 2003, Uranus was in its own house. Uranus is the planet of innovation, and Dhoni who had Uranus in the deepest exaltation in his chart, was chosen to win its first contest.

Did someone mention Uranus is ice cool? Yes, I did. And you know now why Dhoni is too, right? With the willow in hand he turned a typical Uranian, totally destructive in a positive way.

Kapil Dev's World Cup win occurred due to the influence of Pluto. Pluto is a disruptive force that brings in transformation. It gives birth to something. While Uranus makes an existing *something* even better. The Lumiere brothers Auguste and Louis had Pluto exalted in their horoscopes and gave birth to cinema. Walt Disney, who had Uranus exalted in his horoscope, made cinema better with his uniqueness. Pluto's child, Kapil Dev, won a World Cup for India for the first time. Uranus's child, Dhoni, won the first World Cup in its most innovative and newest form.

Unlike other prominent cricketers, Dhoni didn't come from a large city or have any godfathers in cricket. Before he arrived on the scene, cricket was all about elegance and style blended with concentration: slow and steady. Dhoni was all about power, energy and being ahead of the game with smart thinking. He innovated with the helicopter shot and closed games with brutal but calculated assaults. Dhoni proved that you didn't need to stick to old customs to get results. His field placements were baffling for the purists, but most often got the results.

His now famous, unexpected techniques flummoxed his opponents—and his spectators—most of the time. But boy, did they pay off and how! Only he could have visualised asking the unknown bowler, Joginder Sharma, to bowl the last over of the T20 World Cup (that India won) and make a hero out of him.

You call it as a stroke of genius? I would call it a strike of Uranus.

6

The Great IPL Tamasha and the Birth of a Golden Goose

April 2008. Mumbai.

When MS Dhoni won the inaugural 2007 T20 Cricket World Cup and paraded with the victorious team on an open bus, I was a worried man. Uranus rules inventions. It is the planet that loves breaking down old structures and establishing new ones. Call it luck, call it being at the right place at the right time, or just call it destiny. But, to anybody who believes in astrology, it is simply the planets at work. This is what I believe.

Hence, Dhoni becoming the captain of the T20 format was not a fluke. Uranus rules everything new. T20 too was new. Uranus breaks shackles and brings in a new invention or even a revolution. Dhoni, with the power of Uranus, became the first captain to win a world cup in this revolutionary new format in cricket.

My worry was: was this the only major tournament MSD would win in his life? What about the most coveted trophy, the 50-over World Cup? Did he still have it in him to win another major tournament in 2011? Should this achievement be considered a major one or not? Would this victory go down as iconic or would it fizzle out and lose its relevance? Uranus had already given him a World Cup; could it give him another one?

Another thought nagging me was about a missed sequence in the planets. If we arranged the sequence of the cricket World Cup wins on the basis of the birth year of the captains who won them, it looked like this:

1944-1944-1959-1954-1952-1963-1965-1974-1974, the captains being Clive Lloyd-Clive Lloyd-Kapil Dev-Allan Border-Imran Khan-Steve Waugh-Ricky Ponting-Ricky Ponting.

Now compare this with the sequence of the years of the football World Cup wins. It looked like this:

1945-1953-1952-1960-1961-1963-1968-1970-1973; Franz Beckenbauer-Daniel Passarella-Dino Zoff-Diego Maradona-Lothar Matthaus-Dunga-Didier Deschamps-Cafu-Fabio Cannavaro.

I saw that in the sequence connected to football, the flow was smooth from one set of planets to another. In cricket, the years were a bit jumbled, but still all the years had got their due and a World Cup to show until 1965. But after that one astrological patch seemed to have missed the bus—the patch between 1968 and 1971.

I knew this patch was important because in the UEFA Euro, which is the second most important football tournament in the world, the 1964-born Jürgen Klinsmann had won, followed by the 1968-born Didier Deschamps and the 1971-born Theodoros Zagorakis. The 1968-born Didier had won both a Euro and a World Cup. Astrologically speaking, 1971 was an important year without a doubt. I was surprised to see that the important patch between 1968 and 1971 hadn't produced a World Cup winner in cricket. I wondered why.

This patch 1968–71 was one when Uranus was in exaltation similar to 1980–82. I didn't know that Uranus could sometimes strike in the most unexpected ways.

India won the inaugural T20 World Cup in 2007 under the Uranian, Dhoni, when Uranus was in its own house. The very next year, in 2008, Uranus created another magic. It was still transiting its own house, Aquarius, and was responsible for creating another innovative, unique venture which transformed the way cricket or, for that matter, any sports, was played in India—the Indian Premier League (IPL).

You may call him a maverick or brash and arrogant, but Lalit Modi, the first IPL commissioner, should be really given credit for creating this extraordinary spectacle, loosely modelled upon the football Premier Leagues of Europe, with its own innovative spins and frills, which make it one of the most watched sports tournaments in the world.

To know the longevity and scale of any entity, you need to know the date of its establishment. The extraordinary success of this cash-rich league can be attributed to the fantastic date of its launch. On 18th April 2008, the sun, Venus and Planet-X were in exaltation, and Jupiter and Uranus were in their own houses. Five planets in strong positions, what else could one ask for?

The early hiccups and teething troubles occurred due to the troublemaking Uranus being in its own house. The various cases of money laundering, betting and spot fixing can also be attributed to the rebellious, volatile planet. However, Jupiter will continue to make the IPL larger; the sun and Venus will make it prosper and Planet-X will give it a long-lasting legacy. Scandals and upheavals may come and go, but the Indian Premier League is here to stay.

When I saw the date of birth of the IPL (18th April 2008), I was pretty excited and knew that this event was going to be *huge*. I thought I should make a prediction about it. I came in touch with Lalit Modi and told him that the event was going to be a massive hit. Besides our interaction over his horoscope, where I hinted at the various challenges he might undergo during the next few years, I also happened to tell him about the most probable winner of the inaugural IPL tournament. He was surprised when I said it would be Rajasthan Royals. They were the humble underdogs and I had predicted that the team would win.

Even as the IPL was launched, I needed to do an important exercise. Mentally, I needed to slot the IPLs in terms of importance, in comparison to the other tournaments, to know how powerful a captain's horoscope should be to win it. When I realised that the IPL was here to stay, what struck me was that the winner of each IPL tournament would have to have a brilliant horoscope. In the order of importance, I put the IPL in the third place, after the World Cup and the T20 World Cup. Now that is really huge.

It meant that the captains with horoscopes next to the best, captains whose charts showed them fall just short of winning a World Cup, would be the ones who would win an IPL.

With this idea in mind, I started looking at the various team captains. One could make out immediately that MS Dhoni had the best chart amongst the captains. But the question was, could he win it again after having won a World Cup just six months earlier in September 2007? Maybe not. There was probably another captain who had as good a horoscope as Dhoni's, or perhaps a notch lower than his and still had some karmic quota of success left. Also, as this IPL was a new tournament, and was being ruled by Uranus, this player also had to have Uranus in a prominent position in his chart. Who was he?

I zeroed in on Shane Warne.

Shane Warne was called the best captain Australia never had. He had excellent leadership skills; he was innovative; he was a great at his trade, but he hadn't won anything as a captain and, more importantly, had Uranus in exaltation in his chart just like Dhoni. He was the man!

Shane Warne and Rajasthan Royals won the inaugural IPL as I had predicted to Mr Modi.

Every planetary spell gets its due. They have to! One patch that had strong enough planets in it, but hadn't produced a World Cup winner was 1969–71. There were no T20 World Cups available to the gentlemen born then, but the new format in 2008 paved the way for the players born in these years to win some laurels too. The first two winners of the IPL belonged to the birth years 1969 and 1971, Shane Warne and Gilchrist respectively. The planets finally gave their due to these years.

Since then I have been observing an amazing phenomenon in the IPL. The tournament is only won by players (captains) with fantastic horoscopes. You need to be the best of the best to win it; the crème-de-la-crème of the lot. Look at the list:

Shane Warne

Adam Gilchrist

MS Dhoni: Thrice

Gautam Gambhir: Twice

Rohit Sharma: Thrice

David Warner

If Shane Warne was the greatest captain Australia never had, Gilchrist, too, was one of the greatest ever who never captained Australia. David Warner, again, had an extraordinary horoscope and was marching towards greatness before the Sandpaper Gate felled him. Gautam Gambhir and Rohit Sharma were two players who had all the qualities to be great captains, but couldn't lead their country as they were born during a time when the regular captain was in complete control and could not be replaced. Gautam Gambhir was a 1981-born against a 1981-born Dhoni and Rohit Sharma was a 1987-born against a 1986/87-born Virat Kohli.

I had picked out Gautam Gambhir[3], Rohit Sharma[4] and David Warner[5] to win the IPLs much before they

---

[3] Lobo, G. (2012, April 07). It could be KKR or RR; MI, CSK have no chance. *Daily News and Analysis*, p. 20.

[4] Lobo, G. (2011, October 12). Rohit Sharma will emerge as crisis man for India. *Daily News and Analysis*, p. 20.

[5] Lobo, G. (2013, June 16). David Warner is destined to become a great. *Daily News and Analysis*, p.21.

actually did so just like Shane Warne. It is very simple. Pick the guy with the best horoscope after Dhoni!

Well, the worry in this whole IPL *tamasha* is that when someone like a Gautam Gambhir or a Rohit Sharma wins it, ironically enough, they dilute their karmic quota of success (since IPL is relatively less important than a World Cup).

One big sigh of relief from the Indian perspective is that Virat Kohli has not yet won the IPL despite umpteen tries for his club team, the Royal Challengers Bangalore. At least, not till this book went to press. My apologies to all Bangalore fans, but I wish he doesn't win an IPL ever. Let him win one, if at all, after he has won a World Cup for India. What say?

7
Saint Iker and Captain Cool

29th June 2008. Mumbai.

My new organisation was located in the busy Lower Parel area. The many events that happened over the next five years make me wonder if it was karma at play that I joined this company in 2008. It opened whole new vistas for me, directly and indirectly. The region where my office was located was packed with all types of media houses—from print to radio to TV.

One day, in mid-June 2008, when I was on a chai break, I overheard two people discussing the football UEFA Euro Cup. According to them France, Germany and Netherlands seemed to be the favourites to win. I couldn't resist the temptation to interfere. Apologising for barging in upon their conversation I said, 'None of these countries you are discussing will win the Cup. It will be won by a 1981-born captain—and there is only one 1981-born captain in the tournament: Iker Casillas of Spain. He will win the Cup.'

One of them gave me a disdainful look and asked, 'Are you a sports analyst?' He looked even more contemptuous when I said, 'No, I research astrology. I'm saying this on the basis of the planetary positions of the captains.'

The other person, who had droopy eyes, a thick moustache and a saintly smile on his face, told me to elaborate upon it. I explained the idea to him gladly.

He shook his head and said, 'Interesting. We will talk about this a little more later.'

After a week or so, Spain remained undefeated and qualified for the quarter-finals. I saw the droopy eyes and thick moustache again during my lunch break. Once again he flashed that saintly smile at me and called out, 'Hey man, your Spain is doing well!'

I liked that acknowledgement. And when Spain qualified for the semi-finals too, the saintly-looking guy bumped into me yet again. He stopped me and said, 'Hi, I'm Satya Rath. I'm a correspondent with the sports section of *DNA*. Would you be interested in writing an article on your prediction on the UEFA Euro final for the paper?'

It sounded unbelievable. He seemed a saint indeed—a kind of divine emissary at that point—at least for me.

'But yeah, the final decision will be taken by the head of our sports division. If he says it's okay, then your article will be in,' he finished.

Ayaz Memon was every inch a celebrity even then, much before he became the *Cricketwallah*. There was always a buzz when he walked to the first floor to his office. Smoking a cigar elegantly all the while, he would often deliver words of wisdom to a bunch of enthusiastic young journos. I wondered if he coloured his hair and moustache so white.

I tried to read his eyes. If I were in his place, I would have wondered what a young, clean-shaven, bank-employee type of guy, without any usual adornments associated with astrologers, could have anything to do with astrology.

Ayaz gave me his birth details and asked me to describe some past events of his life. I understood he was testing me and, from the look of it, he was satisfied with my findings.

We talked about Bollywood. He said he was concerned about a young actress who had just debuted in 2007 and taken Bollywood by storm. Her father was Ayaz's good friend. She was rather caught up in controversies surrounding her personal life more than her career and her sportsman father was concerned. I told Ayaz that since this actress was a 1986-born, she would be the next superstar, that she would go on to attain the place of the reigning superstar, Kareena Kapoor, a 1980-born. Natural progression, you see, even in showbiz. Besides, she was also a Libra-Sagittarius, who knew exactly how to balance her career with her love-life.

The sports prediction article was published[1] on the day of the football final. My very first article in print. It was a tiny one, so tiny that very few people would have even noticed it. But, I was thrilled. I was a columnist now. Thanks, Ayaz, for giving me my first break.

The UEFA Euro final was played between a young and sprightly Spain and the hardened veterans, Germany. Germany was captained by the cool Michael Ballack and Spain was led by an even calmer 1981-born, Iker Casillas.

Iker had the greatest horoscope amongst the footballers in the modern times. In cricket it was Dhoni. The effects of Uranus that caused one to be inventive and forward-thinking put Iker at the helm when Spain revolutionised the world with *tiki-taka* football. The quick short passes that frustrated the opposition

---

[1] Lobo, G. (2008, June 29). Casillas lucky for his team. *Daily News and Analysis*, p. 19.

involved meticulous leg work. Planet-Y was probably responsible for the precision necessary for such moves. Spain gave six years of unparalleled joy to football fans, but every good thing must come to an end and, in 2014, it did—just as I had predicted.

In cricket, MSD won the inaugural T20 World Cup in 2007. It was amazing that Uranus, the ruler of innovation, was in its own house after 84 years when it happened. It was the same case when Iker won the UEFA Euro in 2008. T20 was the *tiki-taka* equivalent in cricket.

The clue to the 2008 football World Cup win of Spain came from the 2007 cricket World Cup-winning captain, MSD. I couldn't fail to notice the astonishing similarities between our own Captain Cool and Spain's captain, Iker. Yes, Casillas is called 'Saint Iker' for his calmness. He remains absolutely cool in the toughest situations and knows exactly what to anticipate. This surety of purpose and calmness under pressure can only be attributed to Planet-Y. Look at the similarities—a wicket-keeper captain, a goal-keeper captain. Both 1981-borns, just a month apart. One is called a 'Saint' and the other is 'Captain Cool'. That is Uranus and Planet-Y for you.

I have been writing for *DNA* since 2008. The column is aptly titled, 'Octozone'. The 'Octo' here stands for Octopus Paul, who accurately predicted the outcome of the football matches in UEFA Euro 2008 and World Cup 2010. The columns are published either on Saturday or Sunday or before major sports events. For me, lessons for cricket articles always come from football.

8

Dhoni's Mother and the Discovery of Planet-Y

16th June 2009. Ranchi.

Some may find it hard to believe, but I had already envisaged a man like Dhoni on the scene even before he arrived. Between 2003 and 2007 I had researched the planets and the winners of all the previous World Cups, substantially. I felt I was ready to do predictions. I knew what I was looking for. I had some idea about the guy who would lead India's resurgence in world cricket.

I knew that this would be a person born in 1981; that he would be a brilliant combination of the explosively radioactive Uranus and the clinically precise Planet-Y. The fire and passion of Uranus would combine with the zeal and serenity of the newly-discovered Planet-Y to give us the superstar who would win India the next World Cup.

As I delved deeper, a clear picture emerged in my mind. He would act like a warrior with cunning strategy and lightning speed. His strength would be formidable. He would have amazing abilities, the coolness of ice in the face of a storm. There would also be a quirky side to him. Maybe his hairstyle or walk—something about his appearance would draw attention. That would be Uranus' stamp.

By this time, the whole of India was waiting for such a person to come and take the baton from the Aussies. Australians were the invincible force in international cricket. They were the popular bullies of the sport, where beating them in a single match was a task. The Aussies ruled World Cup cricket those days and we, as a nation, lived in the hope that one day a person would come to resurrect our failing grasp on it. And with the backing of my research in astrology, I knew the precise details of such a hero. The combination was magical and it would be difficult to miss. I was hopeful.

Thank God that my man showed up at the exact moment when I needed him the most—in 2005—with his 148 against Pakistan. It was unbelievable. I had done many predictions before about people who were already there on the scene. This was the first time I was waiting for a man to hit the scene and I couldn't believe that he was right there standing before me.

This was precisely the soldier I was looking for. I saw him on TV: a warrior with strong jaws and broad shoulders and that leonine mane! All children of Uranus tend to look different from the herd; they don't mind standing out. The symbolisms of Uranus and Planet-Y were visible in his eyes, his aura. However, a small problem still bothered me for a little while. The next World Cup was in 2007. Would he be the captain by then? I was ready to bet that he would be but, of course, it was difficult to convince others. I remember sharing my enthusiasm with a colleague and getting the response, '*Arre pehle usko team mein tikne toh de* (Let him make a place for himself in the team first).'

He would do more than just stay in the team; he would captain it and lead it to victory laps—of that I was certain. In my quest to find the next Indian cricketing great, when I chanced upon MS Dhoni in 2005, to ascertain that he was indeed the man who would bring a great renaissance in Indian cricket, I needed to verify that his birth details were correct. Aware that the most basic pitfall in making a correct prediction is the correct birth date and time, I was anxious to reconfirm the information on Dhoni's birth.

As luck would have it, one of my training sessions was scheduled in Ranchi, Dhoni's home town. Pankaj Kumar, my colleague based in Ranchi, felt that this was the best time to visit Dhoni's home since he was in England at that time to defend his T20 World Cup crown and security would be less restrictive. By now I was desperate to know whether I was right, and thankfully luck favours the brave (and desperate). We reached Dhoni's home and spoke to the security guards posted outside. I told them I was writing a book on Dhoni and needed information that no one else except his parents could provide and that it was important for the book. The guy went up and asked Dhoni's mother. I was close enough to the house to hear her response through the window. She said, 'They took me to the hospital at five in the morning. He was born about half an hour later.'

Whoopee!

The guard came and confirmed the date too. It was the correct year—1981. Now I was ready to declare to the world that Dhoni was the guy Indian cricket was waiting for. Dhoni is a Gemini-Leo according to my book, *What is Your True Zodiac Sign?* Gemini blessed him with a sharp mind and Leo gave him control over things without ruffling him. The quick-thinking strategist with a regal bearing would lead India to well-deserved heights.

Don't ask me how I spent the rest of that day or even that week. All I remember is a feeling of pure joy and the desire to shout out my thoughts to the entire world. There was no doubt in my mind at all now. When I spoke to my family and friends about him, it was with this conviction. Since they all knew me, they were ready to humour me without always buying whatever I said. Thank you, all, for hearing me out.

I would like to tell all the hardwired astrology enthusiasts that MSD has a Gemini ascendant. His is not a Virgo *lagna* as most of the websites would have you believe. The ascendant sign or the *lagna* is the zodiac sign that is visible over the horizon when you are born. The planets in the first house indicate what kind of a person you are. With the exact time of birth given by Dhoni's mother, the air was cleared about Dhoni's ascending sign.

I do not know if anyone reading this has any inkling about the importance of what I'm going to say next.

I 'discovered' a planet.

Yes. I actually discovered a planet. I'm not an astronomer. I don't have a degree in astrophysics or mastery in astronomy. But I indeed discovered a planet—or a planetoid—relevant and particularly significant to astrology.

As I mentioned earlier, there were 12 zodiac signs, which indicated the presence of 12 planets ruling them. Indian astrology used only five therefore, seven others needed to be added. While Uranus, Neptune, Chiron and Pluto used by the Western astrologers could fill in four more gaps, the remaining three were the planets that I refer to as Planet-X, Planet-Y and Planet-Z.

My discovery of one of these planets, Planet-Y, can be attributed to one man—the great Mahendra Singh Dhoni. Unknowingly and unwittingly, he helped me zero in on that one planet which explained his extraordinary mind that always worked with numbers and always had a plan A, B and C[1].

Now I come to that part where Dhoni played an important role in my detection of this planet. It was his horoscope that helped me narrow down my research to the years 1977 to 1981, when I thought the planet that ruled Virgo was in exaltation. And it proved my hypothesis correct.

Around that time I also happened to study the birth chart of a young widow. She was born in 1981. I could not see any planetary position that could explain her situation. I just visualised a planet in her chart that ruled the house of marriage that resulted in this huge loss. But that particular planet was missing in that particular house. I knew that Planet-Y was present in that girl's horoscope in the wrong house. Dhoni's

---

[1] Cricketnext Staff. (2017, November 29). *MS Dhoni always had plan A,B and C as skipper: Suresh Raina.* Retrieved from https://www.news18.com. Accessed on 17 February 2019.

horoscope helped me know exactly where that planet was if I applied it to that widow's chart.

When I took Dhoni's birth details from his mother and constructed his horoscope, I was amazed to find that this Planet-Y was placed in his very first house. The first house indicates the 'persona' in astrology. It defines who you are as a person. Dhoni could easily be described by the keywords related to this planet. Most importantly, this planet was exactly where I guessed it would be, in the same zodiac sign.

Planet-Y is the 'true' ruler of the zodiac sign Virgo and it is exalted (the best position) in Gemini. These were two of my assumptions. Dhoni's horoscope proved both my assumptions to be true. The widow's chart (and later on hundreds of others) proved that too.

Another important point about the Planet-Y was that this was the planet that gave Dhoni and India the second World Cup. While Uranus was responsible for the first World Cup in 2007, which was in a new format, Planet-Y gave Dhoni another one. Also, the fact that he had Chiron in exaltation gave him the World Cup on home soil. Chiron rules the 'motherland'.

Another chart that confirmed Planet-Y's presence belonged to tennis star, Serena Williams. In Serena's horoscope, there is no indication why she is a tennis player. She is a 1981-born, just like Dhoni. She has an Aries ascendant and Planet-Y is exalted in her third house. Now, the third house indicates the hands in astrology. Why Serena is a tennis player can be attributed to Planet-Y. Interestingly, another 1981-born, Roger Federer has Planet-Y exalted in his 11th house. The 11th house indicates the second half of life (35 plus) and it is no wonder that Federer is playing fantastic tennis even at 37 plus.

After Abhinav Bindra won the historic, first ever individual Olympic gold, I approached him and coaxed him into giving me his birth details. I wasn't surprised to see that the 1982-born had Planet-Y as his third lord (of the hands!). Abhinav has spent almost all of his life staring at a wall and using his hands to send a micro bullet into a microscopic point. There are extremely little chances of error in this game. The difference between a gold and silver medal is almost negligible. Planet-Y gave him the power of winning a 'granular' event.

Later on, thousands of confirmations of the presence of Planet-Y in exaltation emerged in the period 1977–81, using the horoscopes of celebrities and common people. But the first person to give me an inkling of Planet-Y's presence was MS Dhoni. He was the 'King of Details'.

The key words connected with Planet-Y are perfection, detail, granularity, hard work, meticulousness, method, being process-oriented, design, structured work, duty, efficiency, data, analysis, synthesis, etc. I was surprised to find that Dhoni was all these qualities personified in his everyday work.

Dhoni acknowledges that his mind is always bombarded with numbers. It is always calculating, over by over, bowler by bowler. When everyone else is panicking, Dhoni's Planet-Y mind synthesises the numbers and he finishes the game with the clinical precision of a surgeon. No emotions, just cold-blooded calculation. Exactly what Vishwakarma, the ruler of the Planet-Y would want him to do: finish the job perfectly. Dhoni personifies Planet-Y and how! Thanks, Dhoni, for leading me to this planet.

9

Lessons from Tennis

August 2010. Mumbai.

'Bro, you have the toughest assignment of your fledgling astrology career. Boss wants you to predict how many Grand Slams Federer will end up with. Let's see if you get that right. You better get it right and, yeah, also ensure that he gets one more than that bugger, Nadal.'

Derek Abraham didn't mince words—he was very blunt, had a clear point of view and, like a typical Scorpio, could go on and on with a lot of intensity. Linda (Goodman) was right; Scorpios either love or hate things. Derek loved Roger Federer, and anyone who had even an iota of liking for Rafael Nadal would be his enemy. An enemy's friend is an enemy, correct? The boss here was Vijay Tagore, the head of the sports section at *DNA* in those days.

The football World Cup had just ended the previous month and Iker Casillas had led Spain to a stupendous victory. It was his second triumph on the highest stage after leading Spain to a win in the 2008 UEFA Euro. I was trying to work out if Dhoni would win the 2011 cricket World Cup, and Iker's win was a massive boost to that line of thought. And here was Derek asking me to have a go at Federer. In one breath we were talking about three 1981-borns here: Federer—Casillas—Dhoni. All three gentlemen born within a month of each other. All three, the greatest of their generation in their respective sport.

Did Dhoni have an alter ego?

If so, it had to be Roger Federer.

If one was born on 7th July 1981 (07.07.81), the other was born on 8th August 1981 (08.08. 81). We all know Dhoni loves number 7 and considers it his lucky number. I'm not sure if Federer feels the same way about number 8.

When the 22-year-old Federer won the Wimbledon Grand Slam and the world looked at him with great expectations, it triggered an idea. The simple thought was that if I needed to know who would win the 2011 World Cup, I needed to know how big Roger Federer would be by the time he hung up his boots. In terms of tennis, it meant the number of Grand Slams. Simple. How far could he go? Could he go on to beat his predecessors and be #1? Or would he settle down as a number 2, 3 or 4? How much time did he have? How many more Slams could he win?

The top three Grand Slam achievers, when Federer started winning Grand Slams, were Pete Sampras, Roy Emerson and Rod Laver. Roy and Rod both played in the 1960s. Rod ended up with 11 and Roy bettered him by one more to end up with 12. In the 1990s, systematically, with his precise and powerful 'pistol' serves, Pete Sampras broke both these records and sat on top of the heap with 14 Grand Slams.

I was taken aback when I studied the horoscopes of these three men. All three of them—Rod Laver, Roy Emerson and Pete Sampras—had the planet Uranus in exaltation in their horoscopes. Uranus, as I've mentioned earlier, is all about breaking records. It gets exalted in Aries, Virgo and Scorpio. Rod and Roy had the planet in the powerful Aries, Sampras had it in the systematic Virgo and Federer had it in the ferocious Scorpio. Out of the three zodiac signs Uranus is most strongly exalted in Scorpio. Though all of them had an exalted Uranus, the most powerful was the one in Scorpio. So, clearly, the biggest records would belong to the one who had that. The 1981-born Federer was bound to overtake the 1971-born Pete Sampras and the 1936-born Roy Emerson or the 1938-born Rod Laver.

Pete Sampras had 14 Grand Slams. So how much farther could Federer go? Now, that depended on when the next player with 'Uranus exalted' or 'Uranus in its own house' appeared on the scene. After 1981, the year when another tennis maestro was born, with Uranus in a strong position, was in 2002 when the planet of innovation entered its own house. So, only someone born after 2002 could really beat Federer.

Well, that was just a year after which Federer started winning the Slams. What that meant was that Federer would create a record that would last at least till 2035, assuming that a 2002–2005-born broke his record when he was around 30. Now, that record (number of Grand Slams) would have to be much larger than 14. Could it be 16? Yes, definitely. In fact, looking at the fact that Federer had the best Uranus exaltation in Scorpio, he was sure to leave a great distance between himself and his rivals. And, the number could be as big as 18.

While studying Federer and the 1981 Uranus power, I also noticed another crucial fact. The year 1981 also had Planet-Y and Chiron in exaltation. That could mean these two planets, could add more Grand Slams to Federer's kitty. So, could that be 20? Yes, quite possible! Federer could realistically think of 20 plus Grand Slams by the time he decided to hang up his boots! So, 20 was the magical number I ended up with for Federer.

What about Rafael Nadal then, who was hot on the heels of Federer? Well, Rafa too had Uranus in exaltation in Scorpio, but the exaltation was lesser compared to Federer. Obviously, it meant that Federer would still pip Nadal at the post! Sorry, all Nadal fans here, but Federer is destined to be the greatest—as of now. I can tell you that Derek was a happy man when I wrote[1] this. And so was I—since it meant a lot in terms of cricket. It only meant that Dhoni is not done yet after winning the 2007 T20 World Cup. Probably, he still had something up his sleeves.

There was a Queen on the tennis court who confirmed my findings. Serena Williams.

Serena leapfrogged over all her contemporaries. The only competitor she had was at her own home. She overtook her sister, Venus, in due course. Both Venus and Serena were born in the patch of 1980–81—the time when all the three planets—Uranus, Planet-Y and Chiron were in exaltation. It just added more weight to the possibility of a 1981-born cricket World Cup winner

---

[1] Lobo, G. (2010, August 21). Federer will end up with 20 Grand Slams. *Daily News and Analysis*, p. 23.

in 2011. Serena had no competitors and she was on the path to be the greatest woman tennis player ever, overtaking Steffi Graf. The signs were very clear. If she surpassed Graf, she would end up with more than 24 Grand Slams. If Serena could do 24, could Federer do 20 plus? Of course he could!

Now, if that was to happen, the 1981 phenomenon was becoming something large, something really extraordinary, from the perspective of cricket. If I equated ten Grand Slams in tennis with one World Cup in cricket, then probably the year 1981 could produce even two World Cup winners!

By the time the next cricket World Cup happened, in 2007, Federer had already made a clean sweep of an astonishing 10 Grand Slams. He was just 26 and had a long way to go.

All omens pointed towards a 1981-born winning the next cricket World Cup. In the 50-over World Cup held in 2007, Graeme Smith was the only captain born in 1981. Would it be South Africa this time? No chances of India winning the World Cup at all?

I had mixed feelings when India came battered and bruised under Rahul Dravid. While that was really sorrowful, the sorrow turned into glee when the Ricky Ponting-led Australia won the World Cup once again that year. When I researched why Ponting had won the Cups back to back, I found that he had both Planet-X and Planet-Z in exaltation. Either planet had given him a World Cup. I also understood that the timelines of various sports need not run parallel to each other, that is a 1981-born did not need to win across different sports at the same time. But the sequence would certainly follow, that is a 1974-born would be followed by a 1981-born.

Well, that was the only time I was happy when Australia won the Cup. It only meant that there was still a chance for a 1981-born to win the World Cup.

In a dramatic turn of events, the senior cricketers decided to stay away from the T20 World Cup in 2007. Mahendra Singh Dhoni led a young Team India in the first ever T20 World Cup in September and the rest, as they say, is history. Meanwhile, Federer had just notched up his twelfth Grand Slam. I told everyone I knew that India would win the World Cup as the 1981-born MSD was leading the team. They ignored it. No one was focussing on cricket since Tendulkar was not playing in the event. Yet, Dhoni went ahead and created history. His first slice of history. By the end of 2007 the score was Federer-12, Dhoni-1.

Could 12 Grand Slams be equal to one T20 World Cup?

No. Not possible.

Dhoni had to win more. Many more. Federer had to win more too. Then Dhoni had to win some more or another 1981-born had to make his mark in cricket.

And that's when I started to dream.

I could clearly see a 1981-born cricketer winning the next World Cup in 2011. Who knew, he might even be an Indian!

10

The Most Magical Day in the Indian Cricket Fan's life

February 2011. Mumbai.

'Greenie, are you sure?' asked Mallika.

'Hundred per cent. If this doesn't happen, I will stop predicting anything in the future,' I said.

Mallika Vyas, the head of HR, seemed pretty pleased with my answer and gave me her trademark bright smile. 'Okay, *baba*, I'm going with your words. *Chalo*!' She arranged for the screening of all the knockout matches involving India on a giant screen in office.

Though I had been writing my predictions in *DNA* since the 2008 UEFA Euro, the article I wrote before the start of the cricket World Cup 2011 on the outcome of the Cup was very important. It held more emotional value for me than any other piece I had written earlier. As I said, I wrote this article *before* the start of the World Cup. I stayed up the whole night and completed writing it by 5 am and found that it was double the normal word count. Usually, I never wrote such long articles, but this time it was not a standard piece. I mailed it to my editor and went to sleep. I thought he would probably slice off what he felt was inappropriate.

The article didn't see the light of the day for more than a week. I was worried. The World Cup had started by then. I waited for weekends, but the article was never published. Then I came to know that the article had been published, surprisingly, on a weekday. It was a half-page item without a single word struck off, published[1] on 21st March 2011, before the start of the quarter-finals. I was grateful.

While I was happy for myself that I had a huge column published in the paper, I was worried on two counts. Vijay Tagore, the Sports editor of *DNA* had probably taken a big risk for himself by backing a rookie astrologer. How on earth could someone predict such events and, besides, how could one publish them in a mainstream publication? I shuddered to think about the questions Vijay might have to answer if this prediction went wrong. I wanted the prediction to go right for me, for Tagore who had put his faith in me, and for the millions of fans of this country who had waited for 28 years for the Cup to come back home.

But I was very sure. I was excited about witnessing history. I wanted to be a part of this historic triumph when India won the World Cup. That was going to be my 'I was also there' moment.

The league matches featuring India hadn't been easy. We lost against South Africa pretty badly. Who can forget the heart-wrenching tie against England, when the God of Cricket completed his 98th International century, but the team couldn't cross the finishing line?

Did this Indian team have it in them to really win the next three high-pressure matches against powerful teams like Australia and Pakistan? Anyone would

---

[1] Lobo, G. (2011, March 21). Whose stars are shining brightest? *Daily News and Analysis*, p. 21.

have been sceptical. That too, based supposedly on a science no one was sure of. Was that even a reliable science? Could one even call it a science, to begin with? Predicting that India would win the World Cup using astrology was super-ambitious and fantastic at best. How much sense did that make? Was I kidding?

But I trusted my research and gut feeling. I published my prediction on Facebook. I went all over my Facebook wall, writing about the semi-finals and the final.

Those knockout matches were very nerve-racking. My heart sank with every Indian wicket and was ecstatic with every run made. But this time there were more than patriotic reasons behind it. I remember, during the semi-finals, when I went into a pub in the High Street Phoenix Mall in Mumbai, drunk men voiced angrily that India could never win the World Cup. Besides, *no host nation had won the World Cup before.*

Ricky Ponting had been chosen to lead Australia and not Michael Clarke, who was Dhoni's contemporary and shared 1981 as his birth year with him. This was great news for me. Ponting had already won the 2003 and the 2007 World Cups. There was no way he could better the legendary Clive Lloyd.

Why did I think so?

Ponting simply didn't have the planets to achieve that. Yet, the strong squad of Australia was always going to be a threat. I just hoped Ponting wouldn't be injured. If he was injured, then the mantle would pass on to the 1981-born Michael Clarke and India's aspirations could be doomed. Clarke had a great horoscope. It was as good as Dhoni's, if not better. So, I always kept an eye on Clarke. But, as luck would have it, Ricky remained the captain for the entire tournament and India's chances only got better.

Graeme Smith was another 1981-born who was always a threat. In fact, any 1981-born would always remain a threat at any point of time. But when I studied the composition of the South African team carefully, I found that they were not really a threat after all. They had too many players born in 1984. The time was ripe for players born between 1978 and 1981 at this time. So I could safely assume that the South Africans wouldn't be able to cross the hurdle this time either. Their team, under Graeme Smith, didn't have the astrological power to push them through.

But in the final it was India's MSD versus Sri Lanka's Kumar Sangakkara. It was simple. In a battle between a 1977-born skipper and a 1981-born one, only the latter would win. Until Australia and South Africa were in the fray, I was always worried that their 1981-born skipper (Graeme Smith and Michael Clarke in case Ricky Ponting was injured) had a chance.

On the eve of the World Cup final legendary astrologer, Bejan Daruwala, too, predicted that India would win the 2011 World Cup. So did popular astrologers Ajay Bhambi, Premkumar Sharma and Anupam Kapil. Some reassurance! Yes, I did notice that though the final outcome prediction was the same, the astrological reasons they had given were very different from mine. But still, some reassurance.

On the day of the final match, I read somewhere that a few Sri Lankan astrologers had got together to perform a *yagna* for their team's victory. I smiled. Could they change what was destined?

When Jayawardene made a century, I didn't panic. No team had won the final when a member of the opposition team made a century. The past records still disagreed with me, but I held fast to my belief. Instead, I started wondering who the man-of-the-match would be from India. Would it be a batsman, since the bowlers couldn't prevent the opponents from putting up a good score? If so, who would that batsman be who would win it for India?

And then two priceless wickets fell. The Nawab of Najafgarh and the living God of Cricket departed with almost nothing on board. The Indian crowd was in shock. But I was still calm, for I knew this was going to be our World Cup.

There was absolute mayhem on Facebook. Everyone asked me if I was *still* sure that India would win the match.

I posted on Facebook: *It's not over yet. The game is still on—and we will win it.*

I was not overconfident, or confident without reason. It was not just patriotism. It had a basis. It was scientific. It was rational.

Kumar Sangakkara would never win a World Cup as a captain; a 1977-born could never do that, especially when he was against a 1981-born. Plain logic. Astrology is not about lengthy calculations, but about logic. It made sense.

There was mayhem in the crowd, but I was convinced Diwali would arrive prematurely. And with that six over the long-on Mahendra Singh Dhoni made sure it did.

11

How to Identify the World Cup-Winning Team

'Which is your favourite dinosaur?'

I looked up to the squeaky voice that had asked the question.

With his hands still holding on to the Gameboy, my seven-year-old had a part apologetic, part mischievous and part excited smile on his angelic face. After looking at the 'now what was that' expression on my face, he said, 'Okay, you can tell me now or later—after you've finished your work.'

I took him in my arms and asked him to repeat the question, all the while trying hard to think of some names of dinosaurs.

This was one of those tricky questions that Neil loved jolting me with. Some others were like: 'What will you do if you are invisible?' or 'Who is your favourite cartoon character?'

When I told him I didn't have any favourites amongst dinasaurs and asked him to tell me about his, Neil went on to explain why Tyrannosaurus Rex (T-Rex) was his favourite. By the time he finished explaining, I wondered if the traits he had listed was similar to the attributes I usually look for in a World

Cup-winning team. The team that stands out like a T-Rex amongst all the others would most probably be the winning team.

An apex predator, T-Rex is estimated to have exerted the largest bite force among all terrestrial animals. Its power came from the extraordinary body shape with a massive skull balanced with a long, heavy tail and a huge body. All the three body parts were equally important and perfectly balanced. That was exactly what I looked for in a World Cup-winning team, be it football or cricket.

I identify the World Cup-winning team in four simple steps. It is just like locating a T-Rex amongst the teams: by looking at the skull, the body and the tail. The one which has all the three in the strongest positions qualifies and you eliminate the others. The skull here is the captain, the body is the team and the tail indicates the coach.

I know I have made it look very simple though it takes a lot of time, effort and excel sheets, but the steps are the same every time. After you have all the correct data in place, go ahead and follow these four steps and you have the World Cup winner!

Step 1: Check out the horoscopes of the team captains (or the skulls)

Predicting World Cups is the easiest amongst all the predictions, simply because it is usually a once-in-a-lifetime achievement. The captain who leads a World Cup-winning team is treated as nothing short of a reigning deity in his country. So, it follows that the horoscope of such a person will shoot fireworks when you look at it.

The first step is to the find which captain has the strongest horoscope amongst all. I know cricket is a team game, but no team will win unless they are led by a captain whose stars plan to dazzle, so we check the captain first and the team later. The captain's horoscope is like the barometer for the condition of the team.

Now, what constitutes a good horoscope is the big question. If you use all the 12 planets for the 12 zodiac signs and arrange them in the order of importance, and know which planet is more important than the other, you will get a clear hierarchical arrangement of the planets from the one with the most positive influence to the one with the least positive influence. The horoscope with the highest number of planets in the best positions will be the best horoscope. Sometimes you may have the horoscopes of two or three captains, which stand out, and may be unable to decide which is the best. Well, that is a good start. Arriving at the top two or three captains (and therefore teams) isn't bad at all.

Step 2: Check the army (or check the body)

Now that you have whittled down the list of captains, move on to the other players of their teams. Look for players with an exceptional horoscope that stands out and screams at you, 'I'm a World-Cup winner!' These charts sparkle and you should be able to locate them.

Beware of the teams that look strong, but have a captain with a weak horoscope. It may happen that such a captain steps down for some reason at the last moment and another captain with a better horoscope takes his place. So look for all of those deputies and players with extraordinary charts.

Step 3: Check the coach (or the tail)

Now is the time to include the horoscopes of the other people who influence the team, like the coach. He is a very important person in cricket. If he has already achieved a lot of accolades in life commensurate with his horoscope, the team he coaches may not win that glory. If a coach has a fabulous horoscope, but hasn't achieved the greatness he deserves, he is your man. And, if the captain too has a phenomenal horoscope, you have nailed it.

Step 4: Eliminate

Now you start eliminations. Eliminate the teams who have won earlier. I call it the Karmic Quota of success, which is explained elsewhere in the book. There is a preordained limit to the number of accolades you will win in your life. Yes, there is also a preordained set of problems and challenges we face in life. That should be comforting. There is a limit to everything we experience and that can be seen in the horoscope.

The chances of the same captain winning the World Cup again are rare. Only if you see that the person has an awe-inspiring horoscope with the exaltation of Uranus, Pluto, Planet-X, Planet-Z, etc. can you include his name again.

Also eliminate teams that very obviously have weak captains. If the captain's horoscope is weak or if he has won the Cup earlier, then you have a weak 'skull' and the team cannot qualify as a T-Rex.

Eliminate the teams where the captain and the coach combined together have won a World Cup earlier. That is a weak skull and tail and doesn't look like a T-Rex.

Finally, you are down to two or three teams. Out of these there will be one that shines brighter than the rest. Pick that one. That's your team. That's your T-Rex.

Even if you arrive at the top three, you can pat yourself on the back.

I know it is easier said than done, but that is how I do it. Yes, it does involve using many Excel sheets. But the basic outline of the process is described above. I will demonstrate this entire process with the example of the ICC World Cup 2011.

Step 1:

After a thorough analysis, I arrived at the top three horoscopes amongst the participating 14 nations.

1. Ricky Ponting (Australia)
2. Mahendra Singh Dhoni (India)
3. Graeme Smith (South Africa)

Without putting forward too much astrological jargon, let me try and explain it. Ricky Ponting had all the top three planets—Planet-X, Planet-Y and Planet-Z in exaltation—and that was remarkable. Mahendra Singh Dhoni and Graeme Smith had identical horoscopes, with Uranus, Planet-Y and Chiron in exaltation. Both were born in the same year—1981. As I didn't have the time of birth for Smith, I didn't have a choice but to assume that he had all these three planets in the right positions. We could not count him out of the race.

Step 2:

Australia had a fantastic team. The coach, too, had a good horoscope. The core of the team certainly could win the World Cup. India had a phenomenal team too. Almost all the horoscopes from the openers to the bowlers dazzled. I knew that this was India's best chance to win the Cup. This squad did look menacing.

Sri Lanka, too, looked like a strong team, with a remarkable coach in Trevor Bayliss, but their only chance to win would be if Lasith Malinga became the captain. There was no way Malinga would be made the captain in the presence of Sangakkara and Jayawardene. So, I was quite sure from the beginning that Sri Lanka had no chances to win this World Cup.

England could win only if Kevin Pietersen was the captain and, with him being out of the tournament with health problems, the possibility was almost non-existent. Besides, he wasn't the first choice for captain either, with the old warhorse, Andrew Strauss, still in charge.

Step 3:

Australian captain Ricky Ponting had already won the previous two World Cups consecutively, and it would be almost impossible for him to win another. He had finished his quota of World Cup success. Australia only had a chance if Michael Clarke took Ponting's place as the captain somehow. That threat always loomed large in the background, so Australia could never be eliminated from the list, but they were #3 on my list. Australia, with Ponting as captain, was like a T-Rex with a damaged skull. I didn't want them to exchange it with Clarke's strong one.

My top two choices were teams India and South Africa—both led by captains born in 1981.

Corrie Van Zyl, the South African coach, had a good horoscope too, but India's Gary Kirsten had an extraordinary one and he hadn't yet achieved the greatness his horoscope promised. This could be his moment, I concluded. South Africa and India, in particular, looked the T-Rex I was looking for. Complete with a massive skull, huge and sturdy body and an elongated tail. One of the two, I believed, should win the world Cup.

And, this is how you predict the result of the World Cups.

Over to you now.

12

Karmic Quota in a Sportsperson's Life

2011–2012. Mumbai.

As a teenager, when I landed in Mumbai, I realised soon that just a smattering of Hindi would not get me anywhere. I needed some serious linguistic skills if I intended to survive here, so I put in some efforts to learn to speak in Hindi. The constant companions were Kishore Kumar songs, whose clear diction helped me understand the words, and Amitabh Bachchan whose iconic dialogues were easy to remember. One of AB's dialogues that made a lot of sense to me later in life went, '*Waqt se pehle aur kismet se zyada kisi ko kuch nahi milta.*' Translated, it means nobody receives more than what they are destined for nor before the hour they are destined.

This forms the essence of karma. When we are born, our share of past-life karmas—positive and negative—define the quality of our current life. The karmic quota refers to the amount of positive or negative energies you will deal with throughout your life.

When I talk about karmic quota, this is exactly what I mean—the amount of success and failure predestined (at the time of birth) for your current existence, during this very life. Each one of us is born with a certain quota of karma that can be good or bad, and will be resolved in our lifetime. However, once that karmic quota is exhausted, there is nothing you can do to replenish it, at least not in this lifetime. It simply means that one can gain only so much from one's life; nothing more, nothing less. It's preordained.

In the grand scheme of things, people with extraordinary and better karmas are grouped together and are born in particular time frames. Certain planetary positions indicate the degree of magnificence they will achieve in life.

That leads us to the understanding of karmic quota for a sportsperson. For example[1], sportspersons born in 1980, 1981 and 1982 will see successes on a much grander scale as compared to those born in 1977, 1978 and 1979. Also, sportspersons born between the latter half of 1978 and the former half of 1979 will do better than the other 1977–79 borns.

Too technical? Okay, I'll explain it with the help of personalities. Dhoni will have more successes as compared to Virendra Sehwag and Sehwag will have more successes as compared to Mahela Jayawardene. But even Dhoni cannot win more than he is destined to. The quota was only for two World Cups. He has already won both. Hence I wrote[2] in 2013 that India

---

[1] All the examples are generic and/or based on the dates of the personalities involved. Please do not try to copy paste this in your life history!

[2] Lobo, G. (2013, March 31). India won't win another world cup under Dhoni. *Daily News and Analysis*, p. 16.

would not win any World Cup under Dhoni again and they never have.

Also, in 2012, it was clear that after winning back-to-back IPLs, Dhoni could not win it a third time immediately. That was because there was another 1981-born, Gautam Gambhir, leading a team. This was an excellent opportunity for Gautam to open his karmic account as a captain. His horoscope was strong, with him being born in 1981. While Dhoni's quota was being depleted, Gambhir's was yet to be used. Hence, Gautam won the 2012 and the 2014 IPLs.

By 2013, the biggest dilemma for me after seeing Gautam Gambhir and Rohit Sharma winning the IPL in 2012 and 2013 respectively was whether Dhoni still had some karmic quota left to win a couple of other mega events—such as the World Cup in 2015.

If he wasn't winning any more IPLs, did it mean he was inadvertently saving up his karmic quota in order to win a bigger event or had he completely exhausted his quota after winning all of those IPLs and World Cups?

I would know the answers to these burning questions only later. In fact, in the very next month after the IPL in 2013.

13

The Last Miracle of Dhoni

6th June 2013. Mumbai.

The 2013 Champions Trophy was going to answer a lot of questions for me. As an ICC event, it was second in importance after the 50-over World Cup. If Dhoni won it, he would end up being the first captain to win all the ICC trophies. And that would be phenomenal.

I took a survey of his numbers until then: a World T20, an ICC World Cup, two IPLs, and a Champions League. It seemed like a superhuman feat. He had achieved more victories as a captain than anyone in cricket history. If he achieved another titanic win—and the Champions Trophy was huge—it would be like squeezing out every drop of his karmic quota. From India's perspective though, it still mattered a great deal.

I could see that if Dhoni won the Champions Trophy, it could also deal a severe blow to India's chances in the 2015 World Cup. After all, Dhoni was only human. He couldn't win it all. Perhaps he could still win relatively minor trophies like an IPL or a bilateral series, but winning an international event involving all the test-playing nations would be next to impossible.

Even winning the 2013 Champions Trophy in itself would be a miracle. It would mean Dhoni would have to use up the very last of the powers of all his planets. Being able to do it all over again after this would be highly unlikely.

Hence, I wrote[1] that winning the Champions Trophy would be the last miracle of Dhoni as the captain of the Indian Cricket team. Inevitably, it also meant that it would be a massive blow to India's chances in the 2015 World Cup.

---

[1] Lobo, G. (2013, June 23). It'll be MSD's last miracle if India win. *Daily News and Analysis*, p, 13.

14

2014 T20 World Cup—
The Last-Minute Twist in the Tale

6th April 2014. Mumbai.

Sometimes cricket works like the prime-ministerial elections in India. Many a time, at least in the past, we never knew the prime-ministerial candidate until the last moment. PV Narasimha Rao, IK Gujral, HD Deve Gowda, Manmohan Singh are some such examples. It could be someone who no one could have ever expected to become the PM before the elections.

All through this ruckus, the person who had the best horoscope out of all the prospective candidates was destined to be the prime minister, and every force worked towards it. We only came to know about that much later.

Similiarly, sometimes in cricket too a player has such a powerful horoscope that every force in the world works towards making him the World Cup-winning captain. At other times such a person comes to the fore through an injury or non-performance by their own teammates.

Lasith Malinga was one man with an excellent horoscope. He had Uranus in deepest exaltation at

10 degrees in his horoscope. He had the best horoscope to lead the Sri Lankan team to victory in a World Cup. But the Lankan authorities thought otherwise and handed over the reins to a young Dinesh Chandimal. While Dinesh didn't have a bad horoscope, he was still too young to lead the team to a World Cup victory. In a way I was glad when I saw that. It meant that they didn't have a chance to win the 2014 T20 World Cup.

Before the start of the World Cup I confidently wrote[1] that India had no chances to win the event since Dhoni had won two World Cups already and there was no way he was going to win another one. There was no karmic quota left for him for this event. I had zeroed in on two more 1981–82-borns with Uranus in exaltation, just like Dhoni, to win the 2014 event. They were Brendon McCullum of New Zealand and George Bailey of Australia. Both had an extremely powerful Uranus in their chart and either could win.

Unfortunately, India had not chosen Gautam Gambhir as captain, the man with the best chances to win the World Cup. It is amazing how many people's career or legacy has been overshadowed by the towering presence of MS Dhoni. It is not just Dinesh Karthik.

In the 2014 World Cup, Sri Lanka was initially captained by Dinesh Chandimal. He was too young to start his innings and I predicted that Sri Lanka would not win despite having brilliant performers in the team. And then the Lankan selectors had a sudden brainwave. Uranus must have caused it. With it around,

---

[1] Lobo, G. (2014, March 16). Aus, Kiwis favourites; England dark horse. *Daily News and Analysis*, p. 15.

everything happens suddenly. One day, I opened the paper and learnt that Lasith Malinga had replaced Dinesh Chandimal as the captain for the rest of the matches.

Oh my God! What a brilliant plan to fool me! The planets had conspired to keep me in the dark, but somehow I smelt the plot.

Under Lasith, the Lankan team suddenly seemed turbo-charged. They started winning all the matches. When the final happened against India, I didn't hesitate for a moment before coming up with the new prediction[2] that India would lose the match. It was clearly another man with the same Uranus power, who could win it this time. Dhoni's quota was over by then anyway.

---

[2] Lobo, G. (2014, April 06). Stars favour Sri Lanka. *Daily News and Analysis*, p. 15.

15

Why Some Predictions Go Wrong

22nd April 2013. Mumbai.

'Exactly at 1 pm,' Derek Abraham screamed.

'Are you sure? You double checked?' I asked him.

'Yes, man. I saw the ledger with my own eyes. Can you believe this—there were no kids born in the hospital a week before and a week after his birth. Special child indeed!'

Derek also sent me on WhatsApp the picture of the register in Nirmal Nursing Home at Shivaji Park, mentioning Sachin Tendulkar's exact time of birth on 24th April 1973. This was a huge relief. At least now I would be able to work out the reasons why this man was one of the greatest batsmen ever.

Derek was doing an article on the batting legend on his fortieth birthday and he decided to do a special one this time. He also fulfilled my long-time wish with that—getting the exact birth details of the maestro. Every birth detail of a famous personality I get adds to my knowledge of astrology and, without doubt, this one was the most important birth detail ever.

Thanks, Derek, for taking all the trouble. I wish I knew someone as good as you in Delhi, who could have helped me with the birth details of Virat Kohli. The biggest mystery would have been solved and I wouldn't be writing about a third of this book on presumptions.

Making a living on predictions is a tough business, especially if it involves a science which is still evolving—and there are too many sceptics around to accept it as such.

People don't remember the 50 predictions you got right, but they will always remember that *one* prediction you got wrong. They make this *one* prediction the basis for maligning you or, worse, the science itself. I don't have a problem if I'm accused of being wrong regarding a prediction. I have chosen this path, so I need to be ready to face the consequences. But I do have a problem if the science is criticised—an astrologer can be wrong, but not astrology.

That is the simple reason why many smart astrologers take the easy path of explaining the cause of an event or occurrence astrologically *after* it has already happened. I prefer the more difficult path of predicting it before it happens, since I feel I owe this to the science of astrology. This oldest science deserves the attention if not love for what it is.

There are three main reasons why some predictions go wrong:

1. The astrologer's assumptions/theories were wrong.
2. The astrologer's estimate of the timing of an event was incorrect—either too early or too late.

3. The data the astrologer worked with was incorrect.

In the first two cases it would certainly be my fault and I would deserve all the brickbats. If such a situation arises, I identify what went wrong, correct myself and go on with the next prediction.

When a prediction goes wrong, you learn something new and are better prepared the next time. The accuracy of your future predictions improves. The important thing is to realise what exactly went wrong. If you cannot pinpoint that, it can be a problem.

In fact, my own mistakes in the past led me to create my own system of interpreting and practising astrology. Therefore, they don't upset me too much; I gained from the experience anyhow. They only helped to streamline the process.

Let us look at the three parameters:

1. A theory can be wrong or unclear. For example, in the beginning I did not know that there were actually 12 planets ruling the 12 zodiac signs, instead of the five used by Indian astrologers or the eight used by the Western ones. When I got the prediction about the 1999 World Cup wrong, I came to understand the importance of Pluto. My inclusion of all the planets like Uranus, Neptune and Pluto helped me make more accurate predictions.

   Later, I discovered the presence of Planet-X, Planet-Y and Planet-Z. Further, the inclusion of Chiron also fine-tuned the predictive techniques. The confusion regarding why the 2003 and the

2007 World Cups were won by Ricky Ponting was cleared when I discovered Planet-X and Planet-Y.

2. The time estimate can be wrong. Certain assumptions can also work against the predictions. In IPL 6, I wrote KKR would not win, but it turned out to be a wrong prediction. Here's why, in IPL 5, I had predicted that Gambhir would win it and he did. IPL 6 was won by the 1987-born Rohit Sharma. Now, suddenly, from 1981 the influence had shifted to the 1986–87 period and I thought it could not go back to 1981. I forgot that both the 1986–87 and the 1981 patches were so powerful that they could produce multiple winners.

Gambhir had as good a horoscope as Dhoni and he could surely win another IPL, if not a World Cup. In fact, to my dismay, Dhoni, a 1981-born, came back to win once again as late as in the IPL 10. Here too, I got the timing wrong.

It is difficult to be spot on since the events are slightly less important. The World Cup comes once in four years and is easier to predict. The IPL comes every year and is more difficult to predict. What is even tougher is the sequencing of predictions. You need the exact birth details of all the captains in the fray to gauge who will come out the winner and in which year.

Luckily, I have been getting them right more often since my understanding of the sequencing of years has improved.

3. The data can be wrong. Now this is a serious problem and an astrologer has little control over it.

> Finding the dates—the correct dates, mind you—is no simple task, especially when fake birthdates are touted as real ones. Many people falsify their birthdates on record. They shave off a year or two to add to their working years. If white collar professionals can do it, would some sportspersons be far behind? As it is, they have shorter shelf lives. It is quite common in the Indian subcontinent.

Over the years I have found ways to find out more details when the predictions seem off-key. I ask acquaintances and friends who know some of the players; I call the players directly to confirm the details; I ask around. It takes time and energy and can also backfire if people take exception to my questions and resort to stonewalling me. Most players tell me the truth when I inform them of my interest. Here I would like to thank all those sports stars who provided me with their real birth details, which helped me a lot in my research and also in arriving at correct predictions.

I have found some ambiguities and anomalies in the birth details of some of the players, because of which I got a few predictions wrong, or was unable to make a prediction at all. There is a huge difference between what they are and what they are supposed to be—on the basis of the planets in their chart according to their supposed birthdate.

Yuvraj Singh: His birthdate has been given as 12th December 1981. If that were true, then, at least astrologically, he should not have had to deal with cancer. He would also have captained India. As both these things didn't happen, I was certain he was not a 1981-born. Then I met a member of the Indian cricket team (who will remain incognito), who informed me that Yuvraj Singh's real year of birth was 1979. When I used 1979 as the basis for my calculations, the events of his life seemed to fit in much better. I really wanted to speak to Yuvraj's father to confirm the fact. However, when I finally managed to touch base with him and put this question forward, he was very upset and refused to comment.

Younis Khan: His official year of birth is 1977. If that were so he would never have won the 2009 T20 World Cup (and I thought of every other team except Pakistan as the potential winner then). He announced his retirement after Pakistan won the Cup and, when asked the reason behind it, he said[1] that he was already 34 years old and wanted a younger person to lead the team. That made him a 1975-born.

Virat Kohli: He is supposed to be a 1988-born. If that were true, he would be a Virgo-Libra according to my book *What is Your True Zodiac Sign?* The personality traits of a Virgo-Libra surely don't match his. I have classified more than 2,000 celebrities into the 186 categories of personality types in this book. Virat Kohli should have featured in the top-10 names. But his name is absent because I was pretty sure that he could not have been born in 1988, as the official records mention. Simply on the basis of astrology, I would say that his year of birth should be 1986 or 1987.

I called Virat's childhood coach, Rajkumar Sharma, and explained my worry that India might not win the

---

[1] Khaleej staff. (2009, June 22). *Younis Khan retires from Twenty20.* Retrieved from: https://www.khaleejtimes.com. Accessed on 17 February 2019.

World Cup in 2019 if Virat was indeed born in 1988. I hoped desperately that I would get 1986 or 1987 as the real year of the Indian captain's birth. He remained silent for a moment and then retorted, 'So, you saying that we should change the captain to win the World Cup?'

When I asked him again if he was sure that Virat was indeed born in 1988, he was silent for a moment before whispering a yes. Then he told me that he could not continue the conversation further as he had to go.

Well, certain things will remain a mystery forever. They were meant to be that way.

16

The Prediction That Went Wrong

June 2014. Mumbai.

I was extremely buoyant about the upcoming football World Cup. The year had so far been productive with both my big-ticket cricket predictions—the IPL in March and the T20 World Cup in April—having come true. Gautam Gambhir and Lasith Malinga had led Kolkata Knight Riders and Sri Lanka respectively to victory in the T20 events as I had predicted. I was eager to add another huge prediction to my account. I certainly didn't expect it to turn out to be a damp squib. But this prediction did teach me something priceless.

When I was researching the events, I saw the following sequence of birth years of winning captains until then:

1945-1953-1952-1960-1961-1963-1968-1970-1973-1981.

Well, it goes without saying that the next patch had to be 1986/87 isn't it? It was a foregone conclusion. I just needed to find out who that 1986/87 born would be. It would be some footballer whose horoscope screamed, *I'm the greatest!*

Only two footballers could claim to be the greatest of their generation at this time—Cristiano Ronaldo and

Lionel Messi. Fortunately, the horoscopes of both were available on the Internet. So, there was no ambiguity. I know it won't go down too well with the Ronaldo fans, but Lionel Messi's horoscope was a touch better than Ronaldo's. A 1987-born will always be better than a 1985-born. Ronaldo was a great player as he was not just a 1985-born but also a full-moon baby with a few other planets in exaltation too. Hence, he had a powerhouse of a chart.

I was super-happy when Messi brushed aside all the teams with a spectacular display and singlehandedly led Argentina to the finals, exactly as I had predicted. Now, there was just one more match to go. Phillip Lahm, a 1983-born, had a weak horoscope as far as I was concerned and I didn't think Germany would stand against the might of Messi and Argentina. To my horror, after a goalless first half, Mario Gotze just glided a goal across, which stunned Messi—who had been largely powerless that night.

It stunned me too. What was there in the year 1983 that clinched a World Cup?

What I learnt from that incorrect prediction was something that neatly tied up previous loose threads too. I discovered that Planet-Z had just moved over the horizon after 60 years in late October 1983, a few days before the German captain, Phillip Lahm, was born. It was a very recent entry of Planet-Z, the planet of glory. Later on, I realised that whenever a strong planet entered a zodiac sign, the nascent crescent of the planet produced some great people. Phillip was such a product. This patch lasted for just about three months—from October to December 1983. The greatest badminton superstar of all times, Lin Dan from China was born that year in October. A very rare phenomenon indeed.

One important lesson I learnt from football and badminton was the logical sequence of planets and the years, that is 1983 after 1981. The 1983-patch people born after October had the early rays of the exaltation of Planet-Z. This 1983 patch was so powerful that it produced two cricket World Cup wins. And the man who achieved two T20 WC wins was the 1983-born West Indies captain, Darren Sammy.

Now let us look at the sequence of the all the T20 World Cup wins, arranging them in the order of the year of birth of the captains from 2007, when the first T20 World Cup—held in September—was won by MS Dhoni. Ricky Ponting, the 1974-born, had won the 50-over World Cup in April the same year:

1981-1975-1976-1983-1983-1983.

The World Cup wins went to Mahendra Singh Dhoni-Younis Khan-Paul Collingwood-Darren Sammy-Lasith Malinga-Darren Sammy.

The first winner, Dhoni, jumped the gun. Then normalcy was restored and proper sequencing started once again.

Younis Khan (as mentioned in the previous chapter) and Paul Collingwood, the 1975- and 1976-borns could finally win a World Cup.

So, now the complete magic of the years 1974–76, 1981 and 1983 is over. How can we be sure that it is indeed over? Because, if you look at the list of potential captains who may be competing in the upcoming World

Cup in 2019, none were born in 1983. So, we can safely assume that that sequence has run its course now.

I missed a correct prediction, since the event was based on a rare phenomenon that lasted just for three months! Well, that is one more reason why you should be well aware of whatever is happening around you. Every small occurrence in another field can point to things in your own area of a research or answer your questions.

17

Yet Another 1981-Born in the Cricket World

17th September 2011–10th February 2015. Mumbai.

You can count on your fingers the number of Australian cricketers, who are loved by the Indians. Maybe Adam Gilchrist, the only Aussie who 'walks off' after he has nicked it and knows it. Also Brett Lee, perhaps, who played the game with a smile, and even sang a song with Asha Bhosle and starred in the movie, *UnIndian*. David Warner maybe—as the IPL-winning captain like Gilchrist, but that may be past tense now. However, the rest including the aggressive Ricky Ponting, Andrew Symonds—who was involved in Monkey Gate or Greg Chappel—who dropped Sourav Ganguly when he was the Indian cricket coach—are the Aussies who the Indians loved to hate.

I didn't particularly like Michael Clarke, but the reason behind it was not the same as the other Indian fans. It's not that I didn't like Clarke because he had a run-in with the Indian cricket legend, Tendulkar; or because at times he stayed on at the crease even after it seemed he had nicked; or because he had reserved his best days to play against India. But simply because he was born in the year 1981.

Why, my Lord, why? Why so much love for the Aussies?

While I was very happy that India had Dhoni, it was very upsetting to know that Australia had another captain material, who was born in 1981. Unlike in India, we have a fairly good idea about who the most likely successor of the current Australian captain would be. They groom the understudy under the auspices of the captain and ready him to take on larger challenges ahead. By the time the senior player retires, the younger man is prepared to take on the world.

It was very clear from the beginning that the baby-faced Clarke, nicknamed 'Pup', was next in queue after Ponting. Initially, he didn't seem like an Aussie with a 'devil-may-care' attitude. In fact, he seemed far too pleasant to be an Aussie at all. Aussies wear their attitude proudly on their sleeves and he didn't show that demeanour, at least in the beginning. Later on you could see the Ozi prototype in him. Just one glance at his horoscope and it was clear that he was going to go places. He had Uranus, Chiron and Planet-Y in exaltation just as Dhoni did. Added to that, he also had Venus and Mars in conjunction, a very peculiar phenomenon for sports people. A Mars-Venus conjunction makes a sportsperson achieve success after hard-fought battles, usually on the personal front.

In 2011 I wrote that Clarke would go places as captain. This article was written immediately after the end of the 2011 World Cup, since at that time it was evident that he would be a sure shot contender for the 2015 World Cup. And the planets were so powerful that they could surely confer another World Cup—this time, upon him.

As one person could have only a certain quota of success, it was obvious that Pup would have a chance.

Even though Michael Clarke had the same planets as Dhoni, his achievements have not matched Dhoni's as he also has a Mars-Venus conjunction, which makes things a bit difficult for him. Clarke has faced a lot of challenges in his personal life and has managed to come out on top. He had to battle skin cancer, umpteen injuries and a failed relationship. It was his destiny to overcome such tough challenges, reach the pinnacle and win some great laurels. The Mars-Venus conjunction puts obstacles in his path and yet gives him an edge in sports. It's a double-edged sword and he works it well. He was nicknamed Pup when he joined a team of Australian cricketing legends, but has now earned his stripes. His brilliant century against South Africa in 2014 was a marvel of strength and fortitude, for it was later discovered that he had played with a fracture, fighting off the stinging balls from the pacers. That was a hard-earned victory ordained by Mars-Venus.

Clarke seemed to concentrate only on tests and ODIs, which was rather annoying for me as an Indian. Unknowingly, he seemed to be saving up his karmic quotient by not playing in the IPL or T20 cricket. If we compare the big wins, Dhoni has won two IPLs, one World Cup, one Champions Trophy, two Champions Leagues and one T20 World Cup, while Clarke has only managed one Ashes series as a captain. There were no spectacular wins at multi-nation or multi-team tournaments. Yes, he was one of the highest run-getters for Australia. But he still had a long way to go as a captain with a horoscope very similar to Dhoni's.

And that really was not good news from India's perspective.

If we start looking parallely at other sports, such as football, the 2008 UEFA Euro, the FIFA World Cup 2010 and the UEFA Euro 2012—were all won by Spain, led by Iker Casillas who is a 1981-born. Dhoni has won the 2011 ICC cricket World Cup, but he has also gone along to win many other tournaments, thus depleting his second World Cup chances. While football will see 1986–87 borns taking centrestage now, the case will not be replicated in cricket as football is a game for younger people, while cricketers can win even in their thirties. So a 1981-born has to win the World Cup and the only captains I know of who are 1981 born are McCullum of New Zealand and Michael Clarke of Australia (I don't know who will captain Pakistan and England).

Let's see the two squads. Australia has Michael Clarke, Shane Watson and George Bailey, all of whom are 1981–82 born with an exalted Uranus and Planet-Y and almost absolutely untouched karmic quotient. Of the three only Michael Clarke has captained a team to victory (the Ashes tournament). He led Australia to a 5-0 whitewash against England in the 2013–14 Ashes series. He only concentrates on one days and test matches. His efforts led Australia to become numero uno in the tests.

Brendon McCullum was the other 1981-born who loomed large and who captained New Zealand in the 2015 World Cup. He is well known by the sobriquet 'Destroyer'.

Even in sports, where things seem to change every minute, the outcome is always pre-decided—long before the event takes place—the moment the sportsperson is born!

After I had successfully predicted the 2011 result that India would win, I immediately got down to the business of finding out who would win the next World Cup—the World Cup that was to be played in 2015 in New Zealand and Australia.

Months after the 2011 event was done and dusted, I came to know who would lead his country to victory in the next World Cup. My research and analysis pointed towards one man. The man chosen for this occasion was the then Australian captain, Michael Clarke.

In fact, astrology gives you clues to future events much before they actually happen. That is its beauty.

Michael Clarke had such a beautiful horoscope that I predicted[2] his winning the World Cup would be the pinnacle in his cricketing career. And that was as long as four years before the actual event. On the 17th September 2011, this article was published just six months after India won the World Cup.

Let's look at the interesting sequence of events before and during the 2015 World Cup.

Throughout the entire series, at the back of my mind, one thing was always clear—that Michael Clarke would lead his team to victory. Every article I wrote during this period reflected that.

However, just before the start of the World Cup, Clarke was injured in a test series and didn't show up

---

[2] Lobo, G. (2011, September 17). Clarke will guide Aus to No 1 spot. *Daily News and Analysis*, p. 20.

for the tri-series either. There were also speculations that he might not even play the World Cup, let alone lead his team. Even Clarke feared that his career might be as good as over. But not me.

I wrote[3] that Clarke would come back from injury right before the World Cup began. I knew his karma was not over yet. At least not before he had won the World Cup.

[3] Lobo, G. (2014, December 20). Clarke may get fit in time for World Cup. *Daily News and Analysis*, p. 15.

18

The Other 1981-Born Who Won the IPLs

June 2011. Mumbai.

'Dude, tell me, is only one person selected in a particular year to win all the awards? 1981-born Federer and Serena winning so many Grand Slams. Casillas winning both the UEFA Euro and the FIFA World Cup. And will Dhoni be the only 1981-born who will shine in cricket? There must be someone else also, yaar. If it does work that way, then isn't it very unfair?' Derek's question reflected what I had had in my mind for a long time.

Well, 2011 was a watershed year for Mahendra Singh Dhoni. On 2nd April, he lifted only the second World Cup for India after Kapil Dev in 1983 and, on 28th May, became the first captain (and the only one so far) to win back-to-back IPLs. Was Dhoni the only chosen man? Was it fair that he won it all?

The year 1981 was probably the greatest year of the century as far as sportspersons are concerned. Probably the greatest ever players were born in that year and the next, 1982.

Think of tennis and you cannot go beyond Roger Federer (okay, all Rafa fans, chill now) and Serena

Williams. Do you really think the greatest contemporary male and female tennis players being born in the same year is just a coincidence?

If you look at football, the greatest achiever in the recent times was born in 1981—Iker Casillas. Saint Iker is not the most talked about player like Ronaldo or Messi. The players talked about the most in football are the playmakers or the strikers. But there is this bunch of individuals that gains their glory by not allowing the strikers to perform their best: the goalkeepers. It is very tough being a goalkeeper and even tougher being a goalkeeper captain. Casillas had been that for many years for his country, Spain, and his club, Real Madrid.

He has achieved a rare distinction no other footballer has ever achieved before, winning a treble of UEFA Euro, World Cup and UEFA Euro as a captain. He has also won the Champions League for Real Madrid. A great captain indeed.

In cricket, the greatest achievements go to the Ranchi man, the Super King from Chennai, Mahendra Singh Dhoni. His resume looks super impressive. An ICC World Cup, a T20 World Cup, leading India to the #1 position in tests and ODIs, an ICC Champions Trophy, two IPLs and two Champions League trophies. Wow. He has achieved everything a cricket captain can ever dream of.

India's only individual gold medalist, Abhinav Bindra, was born in 1982, with almost the same planets as these other players in the best positions.

I can give umpteen examples like this.

Thus, 1981 was a defining year for sports—for achievers in any domain.

In 2011, my attention was drawn to another significant event in franchisee cricket. Kolkata Knight Riders made the bold move of removing the iconic Prince of Kolkata, Sourav Ganguly, from captaincy and in his place installed the Delhi boy, Gautam Gambhir. This led to widespread protests from the Kolkattans, who pledged not to watch any more matches of KKR without 'Dada'. 'No Dada, No IPL' was the slogan. Despite this melee, Gambhir led the team impressively in his first year in 2011. Now the question was, obviously Dhoni could not keep winning the series every year; he had to be upstaged sometime. Who would do it? Well, who else could do it better than another 1981-born?

There was another cricket achiever, who also had as great a horoscope as Dhoni. His achievements may not have been less spectacular but, surprisingly again, not many speak in such glowing terms about his successes as they do about Dhoni's. I have always found this very strange. I feel that this player has probably been the most under-appreciated player in the Indian set-up.

Well, you know that we are talking about Gautam Gambhir, right?

As a team player he won two World Cups for India. In both the tournaments, his knocks in the final match were crucial, though they seemed to have been conveniently forgotten. Someone else always took the credit away from him. In the T20 World Cup final, he made 75 runs off 54 balls that helped India post a good score, but the man of the match was Irfan Pathan for his three wickets. The match, too, is remembered more for Dhoni's logic-defying decision to throw the last over to Joginder Sharma and his dismissing Misbah-ul-Haq to win the game for India.

Even in the 2011 World Cup, after the quick dismissals of the Indian batting mainstays Sachin Tendulkar and Virender Sehwag, this batsman went on to score a nerveless and classy 97 and laid the foundation for Dhoni to finish the game. But Dhoni's 91 is spoken of with high eloquence, and his winning-six remembered, more than Gambhir's vital knock.

He has done even more as a captain. I could see that he would lead Kolkata to their maiden title in 2012. I wrote[1] the prediction in *DNA*. Derek gave me a knowing smile and a wink when I sent him the prophecy. Yes, Gambhir did it. He united and led a troubled Kolkata Knight Riders to not just one but two tournament victories in the IPL, always leading from the front. He proved over and over again that he had enough fire power in him as a captain.

What I see in Gambhir, and some other players in Indian cricket, is that they could have achieved much more in their lives but couldn't because they were not allowed to spread their wings. No, I'm not talking from a cricketing perspective or even a political point of view. Politics is an inherent part of any kind of establishment. I'm talking purely from the perspective of astrology. When I see Gambhir, I wonder how much India has missed out on by not utilising his full potential.

Gautam Gambhir could have achieved the cult status of Iker Casillas, Roger Federer, Abhinav Bindra or

---

[1] Lobo, G. (2012, April 07). It could be KKR or RR; MI, CSK have no chance. *Daily News and Analysis*, p. 20.

MS Dhoni. Alas, his stature was cut short. He ended up underachieving due to factors beyond his control. If you can see the anger and frustration palpable in him at times...well, it is understandable.

Alas, certain things are not meant to be. Because they are meant for someone else or perhaps something else is meant to happen instead. Perhaps.

19

The Prediction Against a Billion Wishes!

14th February 2015. Mumbai.

The ICC Cricket World Cup 2015 was hosted in Australia and New Zealand, an event about which the entire cricketing world was excited, especially us Indians. As we were the defending champions of the Cup, the excitement of this cricket-loving nation was at its peak. Slogans everywhere went: *We won't give it back!* Hashtags of various types were doing rounds on Twitter and Facebook. Anticipation was visible throughout the nation. Marketers made hay while the sun still shone, by introducing the '*mauka mauka*' theme around the World Cup. And why not? It was a *mauka* for India to create history again. It was a *mauka* to win back-to-back World Cups for the first time. It was almost as if the entire population of a billion would *will* India to retain the Cup somehow.

Is there really great power in collective belief and prayers? If so, we should have won every World Cup in every sport imaginable. If not, we should at least have never lost a single cricket match. After all, we are a population of a billion plus people, and that too who consider cricket a religion.

The World Cup itinerary had been clearly chalked out to offer India every chance to reach the quarter-finals.

Being a country with the second largest population in the world, and BCCI being the richest board amongst the cricket-playing nations, does have some perks after all. India was clubbed with South Africa, Pakistan, West Indies, Ireland, Zimbabwe and UAE! Even if they lost to SA, PAK and WI, they could still make it to the knockouts. It was a win-win situation for ICC as well as for India. It was now only a matter of winning the next three matches. The further India went into the tournament the more venue tickets and TV viewership.

But would India go further into the knockouts? Could they win the next three most important matches?

I wrote an article even before the first ball was bowled in the tournament. It was titled, 'Stars Not in Dhoni's Favour and India is Unlikely to Defend the Crown[1]'.

And, as expected, all hell broke loose.

I was almost called a traitor. How dare I predict India would not win the Cup?

The same people who hero-worshipped me when I predicted in 2011 that India would win the World Cup, snorted at me now. And boy, did they react! I could feel the rage and backlash through their online comments.

Some milder messages went like this:

'Hey, I respect your prediction and knowledge, but I think India will win this time.'

'Don't you think a billion prayers would help India win?'

'Would Dhoni's daughter's birth change his luck?'

---

[1] Lobo, G. (2015, February 14). Stars not in Dhoni's favour and India is unlikely to defend the crown. *Daily News and Analysis*, p. 12.

'I think you are going to get it wrong this time. No one can beat Dhoni.'

'Dhoni has something about him and the World Cups. He will win again.'

Others were less generous.

'You traitor—go and live in Pakistan!'

'Baldie, have you lost your brain with your hair too?'

I had some non-astrological, hard facts to support my analysis. In the just-concluded tri-series held before the start of the World Cup, India had fared very badly. They couldn't score a single victory after landing in Australia in 45 days. It was as if India had forgotten what winning felt like. Indian bowlers, especially, had disappointed everyone beyond expectation. Historically, not many expect India to fare well while touring abroad anyway.

However, India defied all logic and started off rather well. They brushed aside a hapless Pakistan side (thus, taking away their *mauka*) and even beat South Africa emphatically for the first time ever in a World Cup. Against all expectation, India actually became the table toppers at the league stage. And, more importantly, the bowlers managed a clean sweep in every match they played. The factor considered the weakest point in the Indian set-up actually turned out to be the X-factor. And now they were to take on the humble Bangladesh in the quarter-finals thereafter, a berth in the semi-finals was a given. And then, finally, just two more games to yet another historic World Cup victory! This was what many people thought.

Most Indians had probably begun fantasising about Dhoni lifting the World Cup again. But I was cent per cent sure that it wouldn't be him again. Another 1981-born would win the World Cup this time. It had to be Michael Clarke and, at the most, Brendon McCullum. Dhoni—never again.

Based on my calculations I recorded a *YouTube* video[2] and posted it online before the knockouts started. Now this was something very serious. I had put my reputation as an astrologer on the block by going ahead with the bold prediction that India would not win the World Cup this time. In India, a prediction about cricket, and that too about the World Cup, can make or break your career. Yet, I had trusted my research and gone ahead. I had to do it, as I saw this as the biggest opportunity to make the non-believers believe in the science of astrology. Bad news does catch eyeballs quicker and I knew this would too. But I was sure I was doing this for the right reasons.

The euphoria was high, the expectations even higher. I had mentioned in the video that Dhoni was destined to win only two World Cups (the 2011 WC and the 2007 inaugural T20 WC) and he had already won them. His karmic quota of success was over. To win this World Cup, he would have to do something that no human being had done before—beat his karma and his destiny. He would have to play God. I had minutely analysed more than 25,000 horoscopes by then and I was yet to see one man who had beaten his fate and achieved something not in his destiny. If India won another World Cup, Dhoni would just do that. He would be God!

---

[2] [GREENSTONE LOBO]. (2015, March 16). *Dhoni has to play God to win Cricket WC 2015, says Astrologer Greenstone Lobo* [Video File]. Retrieved from: http://youtu.be/7afYpqCg8Jk. Accessed on 17 February 2019.

Alas, India lost the World Cup semi-final to the eventual winners of the tournament, Australia. In the end Dhoni showed that he was human after all.

My video attracted many nasty comments. While some courteous people preached to me about how I was fuelling regressive thought processes, the not-so-polite ones blasted me with uncouth language. So, this being a country with the second largest population in the world has some disadvantages as well. I had done this video, not for personal glory or happiness but because I knew that this was my best chance to show the world that astrology worked. I could understand all the feelings, including the wave of hatred towards me.

I couldn't write a goody-goody prediction this time. This was a chance to establish the fact that everything that happens is pre-planned. Everything is destined. And destiny cannot be changed. This was also a time to prove how astrology can actually foretell events accurately—even the outcome of the adrenaline-driven events, which appear to rely on the abilities of great sports stars.

Who would believe that it was destined in Dhoni's birth chart that he would take the bull by its horns and play that match-winning innings of his life in the final against Sri Lanka in 2011? Every shot of his, including the final six with which he sealed the fate of the match and made the entire nation erupt with joy, was also predestined. He was the Chosen Man in 2011, but there was someone else destined to lift the Cup in 2015.

20

The Cup that India Could Have Won—2016 World T20

12th March 2016. Mumbai.

It was really painful to keep predicting more and more World Cup losses for Dhoni. But, as an astrologer, I had to do the job[3].

sportskeeda

2016 ICC T20 World Cup: Scientific astrologer predicts India will not win this time

Greenstone Lobo FOLLOW
ANALYST

Feature
18.64K // 12 Mar, 2016
SHARE

Stars do not seem to favor Dhoni's luck

---

[3] Lobo, G. (2016, March 12). *2016 ICC T20 World Cup: Scientific astrologer predicts India will not win this time.* Retrieved from: https://www.sportskeeda.com. Accessed on 17 February 2019.

This time around I was only sure about one thing—that India would not win the World Cup. I wasn't sure about who would win it though. Nor did I know how the sequence would pan out this time.

After the World Cup was over, it was all clear. It always is once it is over. The 1983-born Darren Sammy had won it yet again. The German captain, Phillip Lahm, a November 1983-born won the 2014 football World Cup. There were no major cricket captains born in 1983. Darren Sammy was born just a month apart from Phillip Lahm. It is important to note here that Dhoni was born just a month apart from his football twin, Iker Casillas. Greats come in patches. Proved yet again!

A football World Cup comes once in four years. A T20 World Cup once in two years.

So, One Football WC = Two T20 WCs?

Maybe.

But amid all this, it was clear that Dhoni was past his prime and that India was still persisting with him regardless.

We didn't have a 1983-born with a good horoscope—unless you made Joginder Sharma the captain. So, no regrets.

Well done, Sammy and the Windies.

Yes, my mind does toy with the possibility that India might have won this if either Gautam Gambhir or Rohit Sharma had been the captain of the Indian contingent. Alas, it wasn't meant to be.

21

Ronaldo and the Twist in the Tale in the 2016 UEFA Euro

10th June 2016. Mumbai.

The knowledge of who would win the 2016 UEFA Euro and the 2018 FIFA World Cup was extremely important from cricket's perspective. The winner of these two tournaments would tell us which captain would be the best possible to win the 2019 Cricket World Cup.

As mentioned earlier, I arrived at the conclusion that the 2016 UEFA Euro would be won by a 1985-87-born. When I fine-tuned the research further, I could see that Hugo Lloris of France, Wayne Rooney of England or Ronaldo of Portugal could win this tournament. Though in the official prediction[1] I mentioned all the three countries, I was positive that only a 1986-born could win the final. In the year 1986, especially around October–December, Planet-Z entered deepest exaltation in 12 degrees and I guessed someone born in that stretch should win the Cup. I had studied many World Cups

---

[1] Lobo, G. (2016, June 10). Euro 2016: France top favourite; England, Portugal have chances too. *Daily News and Analysis*, p. 19.

in the past and I could see the Planet-Z phenomenon there too. So, I was more inclined to believe that the 1986-born Hugo Lloris would win the UEFA Euro.

Some extraordinary events occurred during the final match between Ronaldo's Portugal and Hugo Lloris' France, which showed how magical it is to see planets at play.

Just a few minutes into the game, Ronaldo, the captain of the Portugal team, was injured and had to limp out of the match. Ronaldo, the talismanic Ronaldo, one of the greatest footballers on the face of earth, and probably the only notable player in the Portugal squad, wasn't playing the match any more. Instead, it was Nani who took over.

What happened next was unbelievable. France could not score a single goal in the match. Ronaldo cheered the Portugal team from the sidelines, and the motivated team went on to score a goal through Eder and won the match. They were the underdogs, but won a memorable night, without their revered skipper! Yes, the history books still show Ronaldo as the captain of the Portugal team that won the 2016 UEFA Euro. Long after the memories of this match fade away, the match will still remain officially captained by Ronaldo on paper. But all those who witnessed the match will remember that it was not Ronaldo but Nani who was the captain of the Portugal team when they won the match.

After the match was over, Ronaldo had taken the armband from Nani, worn it round his arm and lifted the trophy too. But no one can snatch away the fact from history that Nani was the captain at the time when Portugal won their maiden UEFA Euro. And yes, Nani was born on 17th November 1986! Who knows, had Ronaldo played that match, Portugal might have lost!

I always placed a 1986-born in a better position to win than a 1985-born. Ronaldo was also born on a full-moon day, hence he featured as a favourite player in the top three on my list to win the Cup. But, even in my wildest dreams, I never anticipated that the planets would cause another 1986-born to win the UEFA Euro in such a strange manner. Well, nothing can escape the purview of the planets. Things happen exactly as they are ordained.

The UEFA Euro 2016 clearly established that there was something about this patch of 1986-87. More precisely, October–December 1986.

Hugo Lloris, the captain of France, who was Nani's opponent in the finals, was born in the same year too—December 1986. Well, I don't blame you if you think it was just a coincidence.

22

The 1986 Theory Confirmation—Football World Cup 2018

14th June 2018. Mumbai.

Suddenly I found competition for my prediction business from an unexpected quarter. Forecasting had become a big business. Investment banks wanted to showcase their market-predicting tools. They wanted to demonstrate that their way of investing was more correct compared to the other banks. And they extrapolated from it that the sophisticated computer simulations that helped them take investment decisions could also help them predict football results. So, the investment bank UBS ran 10,000 simulations and calculated that Germany would win the football World Cup. Goldman Sachs ran 1,000,000 simulations and predicted that Brazil would be the champions. Alas, if they just added 76 more algorithms to their calculations, they would have got it dead right.

I used 12 planets and 64 horoscopes (captains and coaches) to arrive at France or Argentina to be the world champions in football in 2018. On 14th June 2018, before the tournament began, I wrote[1] in *DNA*

---

[1] Lobo, G. (2018, June 14). FIFA World Cup 2018: Argentina, France favourites, says astrologer Greenstone Lobo. *Daily News and Analysis*, p. 19.

that either Argentina or France would be the eventual champions. Conviction about the planets made me do a video[2] too, on the same subject a week before the tournament.

The FIFA World Cup 2018 was quite significant from the perspective of Indian cricket. In fact, to cricket in general. Or, more specifically, to the cricket World Cup 2019. The outcome of the 2018 football World Cup would indicate who would win the 2019 cricket World Cup.

Thankfully, we can make such extrapolations from other categories in sports. The planets that work in one sport will work in the other too. A great planetary arrangement that makes someone win a World Cup in football will make someone else win a World Cup in cricket too.

When the French team, led by Hugo Lloris, was stunned by Portugal, led by Nani, in the 2016 UEFA Euro final, it was a vindication of the power of the planets. It was a clear indication that the time of the 1986–87 borns had arrived.

The only question was, would it be France or some other country? There were as many as twelve 1986–87-borns captaining different countries in this World Cup. How easy was it for Diego Godín of Uruguay, Manuel Neuer of Germany, Sergio Ramos of Spain, Christian Fuchs of Austria, Igor Akinfeev of Russia, Ashkan Dejagah of Iran, Andrés Guardado of Mexico, Balázs

---

[2] [GREENSTONE LOBO]. (2018, May 28). *Who will win the 2018 Football World Cup? Scientific Astrologer Greenstone Lobo predicts* [Video File]. Retrieved from: https://www.youtube.com/watch?v=QSfxOk4CZjg. Accessed on 17 February 2019.

Dzsudzsák of Hungary, Hugo Lloris of Spain, Arda Turan of Turkey, John Obi Mikel of Nigeria or Lionel Messi of Argentina? The last three players were 1987-borns and the rest were born in 1986.

I followed a simple elimination process by looking only at the captains who had Planet-Z, the one which would eventually make one a winner of the World Cup, in the strongest position. The captain who had Planet-Z in about 12–13 degrees, the deepest exaltation point of the planet, would eventually be the winner. Just five captains qualified that first elimination round—Diego Godín, Manuel Neuer, Sergio Ramos, Hugo Lloris and Lionel Messi.

The coach of the German team, Joachim Löw, had already won the World Cup, just the previous time, so he could not repeat the feat, since there were so many other coaches with fairly good horoscopes around. So, Manuel Neuer was out. Sergio Ramos, Spain's captain, had won three Champion League titles as captain with Real Madrid. This was exactly like Rohit Sharma winning three IPLs for Mumbai Indians. Ramos had utilised his quota of success in winning the three big tournaments, hence another such title wouldn't be possible.

We were left with Diego Godín, Hugo Lloris and Lionel Messi. I named them and the countries they captained as the top three to win the World Cup with France and Argentina being the top two. And France went on to win the World Cup with Hugo Lloris as the captain. Simple analogy, extrapolation and logic helped locate the right winner.

When it came down to a France versus Croatia in the finals, it was very easy to predict that France would be the winner as the previous World Cup-winning captain, Phillip Lahm, had almost the same planets as Luka Modrić of Croatia. So a repeat of the same phenomenon wasn't possible.

Fortunately, Hugo Lloris' horoscope was available on the Internet. He had not done anything spectacular yet with such a fabulous chart and this was his best chance as he had lost out the last time in the UEFA Euro finals in 2016. Also, in Lloris' horoscope, all the major planets in transit in 2018 were in his twelfth house, indicating colossal success in a foreign country. In 2016, the UEFA Euro was held in France, so Lloris couldn't win it at home. He was destined to win it far from his country.

The important thing to note here from India's perspective is that the World Cup in 2019 will be held in England. For all countries other than England, it is a foreign destination. If Eoin Morgan and his men have strong planets for their 'home turf', then they would win. If another country's captain has planets strongly placed in the twelfth house, then they would win.

23

The Logical Next Step and the 1986/87 Conundrum

The 2016 twist in the story of the UEFA Euro and the clear-cut, unambiguous victory of Hugo Lloris in the 2018 FIFA World Cup clearly establishes the probability of a 1986–87-born winning the 2019 Cricket World Cup.

Okay, we need to be absolutely certain. Should we look at sports other than cricket and football for further evidence to confirm this?

The most popular sport we can look at is tennis. One of the greatest tennis players to have walked on the planet is Roger Federer—a 1981-born just like Iker Casillas and Dhoni. Serena Williams, too, was born in 1981. After Federer, the trio ruling the roost is Rafael Nadal, Andy Murray and Novak Djokovic. While Nadal is a 1986-born, Murray and Djokovic are 1987-borns.

Looking at other sports, one of the greatest achievers in recent times is Usain Bolt. He too is a 1986-born.

The learnings from tennis go even deeper. While I learnt from tennis and football and successfully predicted the winners of the 2011 and the 2015 cricket World Cups, now the question about who will win the upcoming three World Cups (beginning 2019) will also be answered by the events in tennis if we can find out who comes after Federer and Serena.

The successors to Federer are Rafael Nadal, Andy Murray and Novak Djokovic. Dare I say 'successor'? When did Federer quit? Well, he hasn't. Dhoni hasn't either; not yet. But it is clear as daylight that the three men born in the years 1986–87 fall next in the sequence. In fact, together with Federer, this group is called the 'fab four'. In this group, Federer belongs to a different planetary era than the rest.

Andy Murray: Three Grand Slams and two Olympic golds

Novak Djokovic: 15 Grand Slams

Rafael Nadal: 17 Grand Slams, one Olympic gold

A total of 35 Grand Slams and three Olympic golds.

In women's tennis, there were no clear successors to Serena visible. Maria Sharapova stood at a long distance. Again, a 1987-born.

So, it goes without saying that the 2019 cricket World Cup, too, will be won by a 1986–87 born. In fact, don't be surprised if the next three World Cups—2019, 2020, 2021, too, are won by 1986–87-borns. By a long shot, there is a minor possibility of the 2023 World Cup, too, being won by someone from the same age group.

24

The Year 1986 and Australian Cricket's Unusual Story

24th March 2018. Mumbai.

I was quite surprised to see Steve Smith going great guns during 2011–14. He was ranked the best batsman in the world, and the Australian media had already started comparing him with the legendary Donald Bradman. But, Steve was born in 1989 and didn't have a great horoscope. How could he be compared to one of the greatest ever? It even seemed he would take over the reins of Australian cricket. I thought if that happened, it might not be good news for Australian cricket. But I could see it coming. I reckoned he would not be able to hold on to the top spot for long—given a mediocre horoscope. What I didn't know about or expect were the extraordinary events that would lead to his eventual removal from captaincy—and not at all in a way I could have ever imagined.

Steve Smith was made the Australian captain in 2015. How could they have appointed a 1989-born as captain when they clearly had two 1986-borns in their set-up—David Warner and Aaron Finch? I was also surprised that the other good performer in the team, David Warner, was ignored for the top role.

I was sure this arrangement would not last long. Maybe this arrangement had come about for two reasons: first, it was a quirk of fate that an astrologically weak player was the captain, perhaps so that some other country could become a world champion. Besides, Darren Lehmann had already led Australia to a World Cup victory in 2015 and he didn't have any chances at an encore. If someone else led the team, then there was a possibility of a win. Now, since Steve was leading, whatever chances they had had evaporated; and second, maybe Australia would have a better captain once again after Darren Lehmann quit. There was another great guy waiting in the wings. So, Steve Smith probably filled the void in the interim and was not a long-term arrangement.

So I thought he would be around only for a couple of years. There was also the possibility that he would be replaced because of non-performance. Then, finally, Warner would take charge and do a terrific job. With this in mind, I wrote an article[1] which stated that Smith would only be around for a couple of years.

When Steve Smith stayed on for a few more years than I had anticipated, I guessed it was nature's way of ensuring that Australia didn't win the 2019 World Cup. Darren Lehmannn and Steve Smith were a bad combination. That was a great opportunity for other countries, including India.

I was happy about that.

---

[1] Lobo, G. (2014, December 28). Steven Smith will become full time test captain. *Daily News and Analysis*, p. 20.

Then something incredulous happened that shook the entire cricketing world. To me it was a revelation of how destiny could manifest itself in an unexpected crisis. It was after all bound to happen. Steve Smith, Cameron Bancroft and David Warner were involved in a scandal that disgraced the game and Australian cricket for a while. The trio was caught red-handed, trying to influence the result of a cricket match by ball tampering. While Warner was penalised severely for being the mastermind behind the event, Bancroft was given a milder punishment. Steve Smith fell from grace and may not be considered for captaincy, at least for a couple of years, ending his chances of winning a World Cup as a captain. This was something I always knew, since he didn't have the horoscope to reach there. What I didn't foresee were the circumstances in which he would lose this opportunity.

The bigger surprise was David Warner. As I don't have his exact time of birth, it is clearly not possible to say which planet was responsible for his downfall. There has to be one planet for sure. Being a 1986-born, he had all other planets in the right positions to make him a great legend, but *one* planet apparently caused the debacle.

I was also surprised that all these events paved the way for one man to reach the top position in Australian cricket—Tim Paine. All of these events must have happened because he was destined to reach the top. Tim had been ignored earlier and would have been forgotten had this scandal not happened.

The full-moon 1984-born has an interesting horoscope that clearly shows him reaching a top position—though under duress—and may not hold that position for too long. I thought he would probably be a transition captain—one who gets the captaincy when the original captain is injured or rested. The circumstances under which Paine became a captain were really unexpected. That's how the planets surprise you. Yes, the exact birth details would have revealed clearer details but, unfortunately, we weren't privy to them.

The way Steve Smith had been scoring made him the best candidate to lead Australia in all the formats of the game. The authorities may have gone ahead and done so and it would have been justified. But they would have lost the chance to win any tournament in any format.

And then the universe conspired on its own to bring the man with the best horoscope to the top. Aaron Finch!

It may surprise many if I say that the entire episode of Sandpaper Gate happened just so that Aaron Finch could be made the captain. But, strange are the ways of the planets. That's how they conspire.

Aaron Finch was the man chosen who would take Australia back to the glorious days. Also, if you notice, now Australia has two captains for different formats, something which will prove to be a fantastic arrangement in a few months.

25

Hypothesis: Virat Kohli Could Not Have Been Born in 1988

Why should astrology only be used to make predictions about the future? Why can't we use it, working backwards, to arrive at certain conclusions and theories about incidents in the past? It can certainly be done.

Yes, astrology can help reveal if an event was an accident or a murder, if it was intentional or unintentional, if it was done by *this* person or *that*.

So, even before we start with future predictions, let us begin this chapter with a hypothesis: a hypothesis about Virat Kohli's true date of birth or, rather, the *year* of his birth.

What I noticed first about Virat were his piercing eyes. His eyes looked into the camera and into yours, as if he would split you open with their intensity. That intensity! It was visible even when he was a cherubic little Under-19 World Cup-winning captain.

What I also noticed was his bling. Yes, he definitely loved showing off. He wore branded clothes, an impish smile—and the brash, devil-may-care attitude shone through.

I love identifying the zodiac signs of people from their demeanour. And, every time a famous personality does anything that advertises the zodiac sign in them, my belief that astrology works is vindicated.

When I say zodiac sign, people immediately think of their sun sign. And, you know what? What you believed all your life to be your sun sign could actually be wrong. The Earth has been undergoing a wobble and the planet's orientation towards the fixed stars that form those zodiac signs has shifted drastically. One zodiac sign consists of 30 degrees and the current shift is calculated at about 24 degrees. So, most people who think that they are Capricorns could actually be Sagittarians. We recognise this factor in India and all our festivals follow this shift in pattern. Makar Sankranti is the celebration of the ingress of the sun into the zodiac sign Capricorn. This is celebrated every year on the 13–14th of January when the sun *actually* enters Capricorn. So, Salman Khan is *not* a Capricorn, people! All those born between 15th December and 13th January have their sun in Sagittarius.

If this myth is not enough, people have another strange belief system. They think people are of only 12 types, representing the 12 zodiac signs! Most people don't know that it is not just the sun sign but also the zodiac signs in which you have your Mercury and the moon that add up to make you the kind of a person you are. Your sun sign indicates your soul, your Mercury sign the mind, and the moon indicates your emotions. The permutation and combination of the zodiac signs in which you have your sun, Mercury and moon indicate your persona.

Hence, Salman Khan is a Capricorn, but a Scorpio~Sagittarius~Aquarius. The Scorpio in him makes him intense and aggressive—someone who doesn't forget a hurt so easily. Think of all those who have hurt him in the past. Even with Shah Rukh, he took five years to patch up again. He is also an instinctive and wild Sagittarian and a truly humanitarian Aquarian friend—a complex mix indeed. Yes, he is not the scheming, practical and manipulating Capricorn.

I have written an entire book on this subject, called *What is Your True Zodiac Sign?*. It classifies people into 186 types, based on the combination of these zodiac signs.

Shah Rukh Khan clearly exhibits the extraordinary communication skills of Libra, combined with the intensity of Scorpio and the shrewd business sense of Capricorn. Amitabh Bachchan exemplifies the perfectionist, a workaholic Virgo with the immensely graceful, charming and diplomatic Libra.

Talking about cricketers, with the giving Pisces and the fighter Sagittarius in him, Rahul Dravid looks every inch the gentleman he is. Ganguly personifies the hurt Cancerian with the dogged and stubborn Taurus. Though the Scorpio in him restrains him, Shikhar Dhawan's leonine streak shines through with his twirled moustache and tattooed biceps. Pisceans Ajinkya Rahane, Dravid and Parthiv Patel are doe-eyed, soft-spoken and almost apologetic about their very presence. Though the Aries in Tendulkar ensured he was an extraordinary competitor and remembered every dismissal and sometimes even took revenge on the field, he remained unfazed and maintained humility due to the Pisces in him. Extraordinary combination indeed.

The Gemini-tinged Harsha Bhogle is always at his eloquent best and another Gemini, the legendary Sunil Gavaskar, could mimic others, a typical Gemini trait. The Virgo, Kumble, could send that delivery 3,000 times at the same spot and the Aquarius in Ravichandran Ashwin makes him try hundreds of variations and even legspin.

When I looked only at the birth date of Virat Kohli, 5th November 1988, I wasn't too impressed. 1988, eh! He would be just another cricketer. Cricket greats weren't born in 1988. They were born in 1986–87. So, he was just a passing phenomenon. Some odd hits here and there and then he might fail and fade away. And, yes, if he was born before 15th November, then he undeniably had his sun in Libra and hence spoke so well. His aggression and passion? Yes, maybe he had his Mercury in Scorpio. I didn't think it was important to look deeper. Maybe, winning the Under-19 World Cup would be the story of his life and there would be nothing more to add to it.

When I started seeing more and more of him, I was convinced that he was special.

Then one day, after many months of 'knowing' Virat, when I switched on the calculator, put in his birth details and checked the positions of his sun, Mercury and the moon, I was shocked. He didn't have any personality-defining planet in the zodiac sign Scorpio. Neither the sun, nor Mercury, or the moon. Can you believe that?

The intense, aggressive, in-your-face brute force didn't have any of his personality planets in Scorpio!

To add to the horror, he had his sun and Mercury in Libra and the moon in Virgo, the exact combination of Amitabh Bachchan, Lal Bahadur Shastri and Leonardo Dicaprio.

Now, don't allow the larger-than-life persona of Mr Bachchan to colour your thought process. If you peel off the superstardom of Mr Bachchan, you will see a sincere, workaholic, non-controversial individual who never gets into fisticuffs of any kind with anyone. And Lal Bahadur Shastri was the most 'harmless' PM we ever had, before Manmohan Singh came along!

Compare them with the confrontational, aggressive, foul-mouthed, menacing Virat Kohli!

Ramachandra Guha, noted historian and writer, wrote an article on Kohli that showcases his inherent characteristics. Probably nothing ever written on Kohli can ever match this piece for the way it brings out the essence of this cricket superstar. *'No one in the entire history of the game in India has quite had Kohli's combination of cricketing greatness, personal charisma, and this extraordinary drive and ambition to win for himself and his team.*

I would say that of all of India's great sportsmen past and present, he is the most charismatic. He is a man of a manifest intelligence (not merely cricketing) and of absolute self-assurance. Gavaskar and Dravid were as articulate as Kohli in speech, but without his charisma. Kapil and Dhoni had equally strong personalities but lacked Kohli's command of words.

Kumble was, by some distance, the greatest bowler produced by India. He was a superb thinker on the game.

Moreover, he was well educated, well read, and had an interest in society and politics. And he was not lacking in an awareness of his own importance, although he carried his self-belief in a Kannadiga rather than Punjabi fashion.

It may be that Kumble alone is in the Kohli league as a cricketer and character. That perhaps is why they clashed and perhaps why Kumble had to go.

Ravi Shastri was chosen over Tom Moody (and other contenders) because Vinod Rai, Tendulkar, Sourav Ganguly and VVS Laxman were intimidated by the Indian captain into subordinating the institution to the individual.

In Indian cricket today, the selectors, coaching staff and administrators are all pygmies before Kohli.[1]'

It is not that Guha found something no one knew before. Kohli always possessed this callous pride about him. He wore it on his sleeve just like he wore the passion to win.

Well, what all of this means is that Virat Kohli is certainly a Scorpio—the forceful, win-at-all-costs Scorpio. But the surprising thing is that if his official birthdate is correct, 5th November 1988, then he cannot be a Scorpio, since the sun, Mercury or the moon were NOT in Scorpio on that day! How can Virat possess those traits if he was born on that day? If it were the same date, but maybe a year or two earlier then, yes, it would make sense. He absolutely doesn't seem to fit into the saintly combination of the Virgo-Libra of 5th November 1988.

---

[1] Guha, R. (2018, January 20). *Kohli's arrogance helps his game but not the team*. Retrieved from: http://www.espn.in. Accessed on 17 February 2019.

If we go to 5th November 1987, we find that the sun and Mercury are in Libra and the moon is in Aries. Aries is the most aggressive zodiac sign other than Scorpio.

Yes, he does have the intelligence and the charisma of Libra and the aggression of Aries. Also, it was a full-moon day. Full-moon days are very auspicious and many extraordinary individuals are born during those days. Virat is, unquestionably, in that league.

If we go back a year further, on 5th November 1986, we find the sun in Libra, Mercury in Scorpio and the moon in Sagittarius. Guha mentions Virat's *manifest intelligence*. Sagittarians are amongst the most intelligent about most things; Librans have style and a fabulous sartorial sense and Scorpios are the epitome of aggression and passion. This combo describes Virat Kohli perfectly.

There is another reason why he seems more of a child of 1986 or 1987. Both the years contain planetary positions that can make someone a great legend. On 5th November 1987 there was a full moon. The year 1986 is even more spectacular. It also contains the groundbreaking, convention-defying planet Uranus in exaltation. Planet-Z too was at the deepest exaltation point on 5th November 1986, justifying the birth of a legendary player. Add to this the fact that Venus was in its own house in Libra and Mars was in exaltation that day. Mars does give him that stamina, strength and brute power and, of course, Venus seems to have bestowed him with loads of lady luck already.

Personally, I would like to believe that Virat was born on 5th November 1986.

Had Virat been born in 1988, he would have had a life and achievements similar to an Ajinkya Rahane or a Cheteshwar Pujara. In tennis, he would have been the equivalent to, say, the 1988-born Marin Čilić or Juan Martin Del Porto.

It is quite clear though that Kohli is in the league of the 1986-born Rafael Nadal or Usain Bolt or maybe the 1987-born Novak Djokovic or Lionel Messi. He certainly isn't comparable to an Agüero, a Čilić or a Del Porto.

Something is wrong somewhere.

If Virat Kohli was indeed born in 1986 or 1987, then we Indians have a cricketing equivalent of a Messi/ Usain Bolt/Rafael Nadal!

That would be great news for India. By the stratospheric fame and value attached to his name and the legend in the making that he is, it is very clear as daylight that Virat indeed was born either in 1986 or 1987.

26

Just Before the Predictions...

Hopefully, you have read the preceding chapters which show the logic I use before I hazard a prediction. Now, we will get into the actual predictions. Let me take a moment here to explain the arrangement of these predictions. In continuation of the linear structure of the book, the predictions too have been listed in a chronological order.

The immediate interest and focus is on the upcoming ICC World Cup in 2019, so the first few predictions are on that subject. Following this are some upcoming popular cricket events—like the 2020 T20 World Cup, and India's tour to South Africa and to Australia again. The next set of predictions are about male and female cricketers, arranged chronologically, starting from the oldest to the youngest. Well, in some cricketers' case, you may wonder if the birthdate/chronology is incorrect. Well, in that case you will have to go back to the chapter and read the explanation behind it.

Some of these cricketers have either already retired or are about to—and we shall look at their future. Some of them are in the current cricket squad and we shall look at their immediate and long-term future. Then, we shall focus on the future superstars of cricket, the young upcoming stalwarts. Finally, we shall look into the distant future and try to decipher what is in store for Indian cricket.

We will close the predictions with a focus on a few administrators. After the predictions, there is a bonus chapter on some tips for IPL team owners and talent scouts.

Cricket is a religion in India and I'm amazed at the way some people rattle off statistics connected to cricketers. Most of these predictions are answers to questions people have posed to me directly over time, or some enthusiactic cricket fans on various forums.

Prediction #1

Can India Win a World Cup Now with Dhoni in the Squad?

'*Yenna idu, Neenga namma thalaivara paththi appadi eppadi ezhuthalam?*' ('How can you write about our *thalaivar* (leader) like this?') A participant in my training programme, conducted in Chennai, confronted me. Tamilians just love their heroes. They can be from the film world, politics or cricket. Mahendra Singh Dhoni was now the hero of Tamil Nadu and no self-respecting Tamilian liked the '*thalaivar*' Dhoni being ridiculed. They wanted their heroes to be on top forever.

One of my articles annnouncing that the Chennai Super Kings would not remain the King any more had angered the Chennaiite. Even otherwise, it usually takes me a lot to pacify my Tamil friends when I say something negative about Dhoni. Moreover, they cannot see another Tamilian ridiculing their 'Tamil' hero. Yes, now Dhoni was no more the child of Jharkhand. Tamilians considered him their own.

Mahendra Singh Dhoni is arguably the best captain India has ever had. And, statistically, he is the most successful captain ever, especially when it involves the ICC tournaments. He is also the greatest ever finisher India has produced in limited-overs cricket. Actually, in any form of cricket. And, yes, he has earned the right to bow out when *he* feels it is the right time to call it quits. Whenever he does, the entire nation will bid him a teary farewell. It will be as poignant a moment as we witnessed when Sachin Tendulkar retired.

It seems Dhoni is targeting the picturesque Lords to announce his retirement, that is, assuming India reaches the finals of the 2019 World Cup.

I presume many *Thalaivar* fans are also fantasising about the special moment in 2011 being repeated in 2019—Dhoni hitting a six and winning the World Cup. But that will not happen. Dhoni is not going to hit a six to seal another World Cup win.

The best phase in Dhoni's career finished in 2016 when Planet-X entered his twelfth house—the house of losses. In fact, astrologically speaking, everything after that has been a bonus and now, unfortunately, what we see is the tail end of Dhoni's long and amazing innings.

I have utmost respect for Dhoni the batsman, the ambassador for cricket, the ice-cool captain and probably the best '*thalaivar*' India has ever had. However, even though I may not like it much myself, I need to speak objectively from the perspective of an Indian astrologer—and I can see that Dhoni's presence in the 2019 Indian squad could well rob India of another great chance to win a World Cup.

Die-hard fans of Dhoni would point out his extraordinary form in the 2018 IPL and his recent superb run in one-day matches in Australia and New Zealand in 2018–19. Good Lord, he even won the man-of-the-tournament award in the Australia series and you're still counting him out? He has won a few matches under his own steam. His winning streak is intact. He is a lucky mascot for his team. His history with World Cups is well known. How can you not have him in the team that is World Cup bound? Besides, who is there to replace him anyway?

Trust me, I'm not bothered about the debate regarding whether Dhoni has lost his reflexes or not. I'm not concerned that the famous helicopter shots have disappeared or that his ability to finish off games has waned in the recent times. Nor do I panic when I see him accumulating runs painfully in ones and twos, boundaries being few and far between. I know that all these things don't matter. I know that when a person is destined to win, all the talk about form and ability won't matter. Whoever is destined to win will win—all adverse factors notwithstanding. The biggest question that bothers me is: according to astrology, does Dhoni still have a ghost of a chance to win another World Cup?

If not, then despite his now-hot now-cold form, the BCCI will stick to their guns, take Dhoni along with them and play him in all the matches. Ravi Shastri will give the camera his mock-serious look, thunder that India has everything under control and express his confidence in Dhoni. Virat will probably wonder what he is doing and agree half-heartedly with that decision. If that happens, you can be sure of one thing—India will not win the 2019 World Cup.

Virat Kohli put his foot down and ensured that Yuvraj and Gambhir were not in the squad any more. It is not really surprising that he didn't do the same for Dhoni. It is not entirely his fault though. Dhoni's the captain he's played under and probably been 'groomed' and 'trained' to quite an extent. Plus he takes advice from him now and then as the former captain. It's not really surprising that he'd be hesitant to do this. Besides, there aren't enough finishers in Indian cricket today. Who next after Dhoni? No one—at least as far as the eye can see.

Some articles suggest that Dhoni should be in the team even if only as a mentor to the youngsters. Even Kohli looks towards him for many decisions upon the field. Now, that is ludicrous. It is a sport. No one can be a passenger. Everyone has to drive and pedal. But Dhoni is not just the wicket-keeper, even if that part of him is still sublime. His main role is that of the finisher and that is where India may just slip up.

The boy, who recently stepped out of his teens, and has enough spunk in him, another wicket-keeper-batsman, Rishabh Pant, is still too wet behind the ears to be trusted with the role of a finisher. There are, however, many names like Dinesh Karthik, Ambati Rayudu or even Sanju Samson, who could be entrusted with that role. But the BCCI and the powers-to-be probably believe that Dhoni is their man and all the others—the younger crop—can wait.

Personally, I feel the best man to replace MS Dhoni would be Ambati Rayudu or Dinesh Karthik (both 1985-born). Ambati has sizzled in the recent times and shown that he has a lot of mettle. The modest Karthik, who played a Dhoni to win the 2018 Nidahas Trophy final against Bangladesh with a last-ball six, said that he was a student in the university of cricket (probably referring to Dhoni's finishing skills) where Dhoni was the topper. But it seems this student has come of age and is ready for the exams as the topper has already passed out of college.

The astrological reason why Dinesh or Ambati should replace Dhoni? Cricketing pundits would say, a like replacement, a younger replacement, a replacement for someone who is over the hill and so on. I, on the other hand, would simply say that we should replace Dhoni with Dinesh or Ambati, because these two have a far better horoscope—at this moment—than Dhoni. Karthik and Ambati will probably never be as great as Dhoni, but these two are the best fit *right now* to replace him.

After the recently concluded Asia Cup and the series against West Indies in 2018 and the series down under in 2018–19, Ambati has more or less sealed his spot in the #4 position. Now, bring in Dinesh Karthik in place of Dhoni and we are sorted. Even if Dinesh fails in a few matches, it is alright; he still has the ability to be a match winner at an important stage in the World Cup. With Dinesh we have a chance; with Dhoni we have none.

Dhoni has achieved everything to be achieved in cricket. He has won three ICC trophies as a captain—the ICC 2007 T20 World Cup, the ICC 2011 World Cup and the ICC Champions Trophy 2013. Mind you, he contributed a great deal in all of them as a batsman too.

I have said this before several times over—Dhoni's best is over. And I stand by that. He has squeezed out the last drop of luck by winning the 2018 IPL. Now, at least according to astrology, he cannot win any more. If he is in the Indian XI in the final against England at Lords on 14th July 2019, it seems quite certain that he would not end up on the winning side. Dhoni batted well and finished games in Australia and New Zealand in 2018–19. But he will just not be able to do that if India plays England in the final of the World Cup in 2019. Why? Because he is not destined for another MOM award in the final of a World Cup. It would not be a big loss for him, but a huge opportunity lost for all the other ten players in the team.

Planet-X and Planet-Z are two planets that will be in the strongest positions during May–July 2019, when the tournament is being played. Both these planets are in the weakest positions in Dhoni's birth chart and they will be transiting into his twelfth house—the house of losses. The twelfth house in astrology also stands for foreign countries. This could literally translate as 'losses in a foreign land'.

Mind you, it is not about his form or anything. He may even end up hitting a century or take five catches in the final match, but he will still end up on the losing side. Unfortunately, that is how the planets work.

Waqt se pehle, aur kismet se zyada kisiko kuch nahi milta.

Dhoni always had the kismet (luck), but *now* is not his *waqt* (time).

Prediction #2

Can India Win the 2019 ICC Cricket World Cup?

In India, there are exactly 7,245,986 cricket experts who could tell you who will win the World Cup in 2019. Yes, believe me, I have actually counted them. Okay, just kidding. While all these experts will tell you the cricketing logic behind their pick for the winner, I would like to tell you the astro-logic behind my choices.

I know this is the chapter you wanted to rush to and read first. But I didn't want to give you the prediction directly. I wanted to present to you the logic behind it. But we need data to arrive at logic. In all these preceding chapters I was trying to build up to the logic so that *we* can finally predict the winner. Yes, *we*! You and I put together. Let us see if *we* can crack this.

So, amongst the top teams competing, which one looks like a Tyrannosaurus Rex to you?

Which team has the capacity to go down as the *Sholay* team and win the World Cup? What does *your* astro-logic say based on all that you have read so far?

1. India under Virat Kohli
2. England under Eoin Morgan
3. Australia under Aaron Finch
4. South Africa under Faf du Plessis

Any cricket expert, even your next door one, could tell you these are the four teams that have the most chances of reaching the semi-finals of the marquee event in 2019. Some keen observers would say Pakistan may replace one of the above teams, depending upon which Pakistan turns up in the event—this one being the most unpredictable team, especially when it comes to the World Cups.

But regardless of whatever the experts tell you, believe me, astrologically there are only two teams that have a chance to win this World Cup. Just two teams!

If you have read all the preceding chapters carefully, you would know the names even before I spell them out. Before I do that, as discussed elsewhere, let's follow the four-step process to find out who will win the World Cup in 2019.

Step 1: Check out the horoscopes of the team captains (or the skulls)

Arranging the teams on the basis of the strength of the captain's horoscope.

I have arranged the top eight teams, from an astrological perspective, from the best to the one with the least chances. As of now—the moment I am writing this, these are the probable captains for the World Cup. But a couple of changes cannot be ruled out.

1. England: Eoin Morgan
2. Australia: Aaron Finch
3. India: Virat Kohli
4. South Africa: Faf Du Plessis
5. Pakistan: Sarfraz Ahmed
6. Bangladesh: Shakib-Al-Hasan
7. New Zealand: Kane Richardson

8. Sri Lanka: Dinesh Chandimal/Lasith Malinga
9. West Indies: Jason Holder

The reason for this ranking is based on the fact that the 2019 World Cup will be won by a captain born in the years 1986–87. The top three teams have captains who were born in the years 1986–87. Faf Du Plessis has a good horoscope, but it is not good enough. It's amazing how South Africa continue to select captains who have 'nearly there' horoscopes. Though the 1990-born New Zealand captain has a good horoscope, it is too early for him yet to win the tournament. Who will captain Sri Lanka isn't very clear as of now. The only person who has any chance of leading the Lankans to a World-Cup victory, the 1987-born Angelo Mathews, doesn't seem to be in the good books of the selectors. If it is the 1989-born Dinesh Chandimal, then they have no chance at all. Lasith Malinga has already reaped all the benefits of his horoscope and he cannot create any further magic, if chosen as captain. The Pakistan team, too, looks good. But it has no chance to win the Cup, as Sarfraz's biggest success was supposed to be the Champions's Trophy that he won in 2017. The Pakistani head of the T-Rex is a bit skewed due to this win. Bangladesh's captain, Shakib, was born in 1987 and has a great horoscope. Yes, the skull of the Bangladeshi T-Rex does look good.

Eoin Morgan and Aaron Finch have the best horoscopes amongst the captains and Kohli's is no less. The England captain, Eoin Morgan, has never achieved a great win so far in his career, despite having a horoscope similar to the Olympic gold medalist, Usain Bolt (who has won several medals). This could be Eoin's best chance to rectify that. And where else than on the highest stage amongst the cricket pantheon? Giving England a tough fight is Aaron Finch's Australia. The Sandpaper Gate was the best thing that could have happened to them. If that had not happened, Steven Smith would have remained the captain and Darren Lehmann the coach. Both of them had no chance to win the Cup. But, with Aaron Finch born on a full-moon day, Australia is going to be a big threat. Don't read too much into the test and ODI losses of Australia to India in 2018–19. This Aussie team can easily make a huge comeback. India's captain, Virat Kohli, has a superb horoscope too (the 1986 version); one of the best captains in the fray if not the best. So, in the first step, England, Australia and India emerge the top three T-Rex heads.

Step 2: Check the army (or the body)

Undoubtedtly, the English team looks the best in terms of the players. What a team! Look at them. They have five players who were born in 1990, who may be a part of the playing XI, and at least two 1986–87 borns. The rest of the players, too, seem to have the best planets in place. This England team looks the strongest at the moment to win their first ever World Cup. This looks like the ideal *Sholay* team to me. The greatest starcast to ever assemble for England in a World Cup.

Australia lurks large with Warner and Smith set to return for the World Cup. Their opening pair of Finch and Warner has been effective and has won a World Cup earlier. They might do it yet gain. The addition of players like Travis Head, Chris Lynn and D'Arcy Short would add more might to their team. The only factor that goes against them is that they won the last World Cup and about five-six players in the playing XI would have been a part of the previous World Cup victory and, hence, their karmic quota might be a bit shrunk.

The Sri Lankan team is good, if a tad low on confidence after the exodus of talent from their set-up. They cannot win this 2019 edition for sure. But they could try to create some upsets. Pakistan has a good, young squad. Expect them to cause a few upsets. The body looks strong. Bangladesh has a set of players with mediocre horoscopes. They don't look strong enough to beat the top teams to win the Cup.

India does have a good team, even if a bit short of players born in the 1990s. But, nevertheless, a good bunch indeed. The biggest flaw of the Indian team, as everyone knows by now, even without astrology, is their middle order and the lack of finishers. Dhoni isn't going to do it again. The body of the Indian T-Rex looks malnourished. This may have a telling effect on the results. The body looks uneven with the addition of players either too young—like Rishabh Pant and Khaleel Ahmed, or too old—like Kedar Jadhav and MS Dhoni—in the playing XI. If India won't play Dinesh Karthik, we lose even more chances. K.L. Rahul has a great horoscope but his best of times would come only in the 2020s. Vijay Shankar is not exactly going through a good patch astrologically right now. Ashwin will be absent anyway, so some chances may be lost there too. India hasn't found the right mix of players in the right age group to win a World Cup. So, the T-Rex with the best body seems to be that of England, followed by Pakistan and Australia. India may end up with a badly damaged body if they are not careful.

Here's a comparative chart of the most likely playing XI to represent each country. This is based on the commonest slot each player has played in over the last year and seems the most likely to be fielded by the

Slot	Australia	Birthdate	England	Birthdate	India	Birthdate
Opener 1	Aaron Finch ©	17-Nov-1986	Jason Roy	21-Jul-1990	Rohit Sharma	30-Apr-1987
Opener 2	David Warner	27-Oct-1986	Jonny Bairstow/ Alex Hales	1989	Shikhar Dhawan/K.L. Rahul	1985/ 1992
#3	Steven Smith	2-June-1989	Joe Root	30-Dec-1990	Virat Kohli©	5-Nov-1986
#4	Shaun Marsh/ Travis Head	1983/ 1993	Eoin Morgan©	10-Sep-1986	Ambati Rayudu/ Rishabh Pant	1985/ 1997
#5	Glenn Maxwell/ Chris Lynn	1988/ 1990	Ben Stokes	4-June-1991	Kedar Jadhav/ Vijay Shankar/ Dinesh Karthik	1985/ 1991
Wicket Keeper	Alex Carey	27-Aug-1991	Jos Buttler	08-Sep-1990	M.S Dhoni	7-Jul-1981

Slot	Australia	Birthdate	England	Birthdate	India	Birthdate
All Rounder	Mitchell Marsh	20-Oct-1991	Moeen Ali	18-June-1987	Hardik Pandya	11-Oct-1993
#8	Pat Cummins	08-May-1993	Chris Woakes	02-Mar-1989	Bhuv Kumar/ Siddarth Kaul	1990
#9	Nathan Lyon	20-Nov-1987	Mark Wood/ Dawson	1990	Yuzvendra Chahal/ Kuldeep Yadav	1990/ 1994
#10	Mitchel Starc	30-Jan-1990	Adil Rashid/ Joe Denly	1988/ 1986	Mohd Shami	3-Sep-1990
#11	Josh Hazlewood	8-Jan-1991	Jake Ball/ Willey/ Curran/ Stone	1990/95/93	Jasprit Bumrah	06-Dec-1993

respective countries. In case of Australia, you know that they were missing the duo very badly and they will walk straight back to their slots.

It is very unfortunate that India has a pool of senior players who have already exhausted their karmic quota of success or younger players whose best times are yet to come.

In case Jos Buttler teams up with Jason Roy, it would be the most potent opening pair in the competition. In the last World Cup, won by Australia, the opening pair was Aaron Finch and David Warner, both 1986-borns. The year 1990 is the most important after 1986–87 and, this time, if England has two 1990-borns at the top, it could be a devastating factor for the other teams. It is scary to see that England has a 1986, 1990 or a 1993-born replacement for every slot. If the 1986-born Joe Denly replaces one of the spinners down the order, he can add to their might. Joe Root, a 1990-born, may just end up being the highest scorer for England, if not overall. Jason Roy and Jos Buttler could do that too. Expect some 1990-born bowler to be the highest wicket-taker too.

There is one player in the England team who has a badly placed Planet-X. That planet took him to the wrong side of the law once and he has already seen the worst as a result. The only blemish has now been removed and he is a free man now. Well, I'm talking about the all-rounder Ben Stokes. Overall, every member in the England team looks overwhelming. The bowlers are either 1987 or 1989-91 born, adding to the strength of the team. The country where cricket originated has never won a World Cup. This team seems to be the one that can finally make it happen. The English body of the T-Rex looks the most menacing.

Step 3: Check the coach (or the tail)

While England has two bases well covered—the captain and the team—the coach is suspect as he has already won two IPLs and one Big Bash League. Does he still have any karmic quota left to win another one? Yes. Well...almost. Trevor Bayliss, the England coach, has not won any laurels as a player, which works in his favour. Bayliss has a great horoscope and hence he may have some karmic quota left to win another huge tournament. Just because he has won a few major tournaments before, England loses half a point here. Their dinosaur has a slightly weak tail. But the body and the head are super strong and a slightly dented tail shouldn't be a hindrance.

Australia has a very good tail with their coach, Darren Lehmann, paving the way for Justin Langer. Langer has the best horoscope amongst all the coaches in the fray and it looks like he is sure to win a World Cup for them. Will it be this time? Well, maybe. They will have to cross the biggest barrier in England for that.

India seriously doesn't have a great tail. Ravi Shastri has already been there, done that; he has squeezed out all the possibilities as a player and then as a coach. By winning the test series in Australia in 2018–19 for the first time, Shastri has extracted the biggest victory of his career. Now, winning a World Cup would be a far-fetched idea. Anil Kumble would have been the best bet for India but, alas, that is a different story altogether.

Pakistan doesn't have a good tail in Mickey Arthur, who has already won a Champions Trophy. Bangladesh coach's horoscope doesn't inspire much confidence either. Sri Lanka does have a good coach, which means the Lankan T-Rex has a good tail!

Step 4: Eliminate

Pakistan is out of the race. The reason is simple. Sarfraz Ahmed has already won the Champions Trophy in 2017 with the same coach. The CT is the second most important trophy of the ICC and, now, it won't be possible for Pakistan to win another one immediately. Besides, Sarfraz has tough competition in Eoin Morgan, Virat Kohli and Aaron Finch, who have better horoscopes than him.

Mark my words, the Sri Lankan team under Dinesh Chandimal, has the ability to rise from the ashes. Their coach, Chandika Hathurasinghe, has an extraordinary horoscope and will engineer a great turnaround. They, undoubtedly, have the firepower to do well in the future. *This time* they might miss out though. Bangladesh just has a good skull and that won't be enough.

So, the top two teams, according to me, after the complete analysis of all the T-Rexes are:

1. England
2. Australia

Yes, England have the best chances to win the tournament. They look like a real T-Rex with a great head, a fantastic body and a decent tail. England seems to have that set of players who can go on to be folklore heroes, crafting the first ever cricket World Cup win for their country. I will be really surprised if they don't win it this time. It will take a miracle for any other team to win the Cup.

If England doesn't, then Australia should win it. Only Aaron Finch can perform that miracle of beating England. With difficulty I stopped myself from proclaiming that England will be the country to win this World Cup. However, an almost-as-good Australia may pip England at the post. If England and Australia play the finals on the 14th of July 2019 at Lords, I would say that the match would be 75:25 in favour of England. If any other team plays England in the final, then the ratio would be 100:0. England should be one of the finalists for sure.

It pains me to say this, but India seems to have no chances to win the 2019 World Cup, unfortunately. We have the best captain possible, but not having the best set of players, and a weak coach, will cost us the Cup. Sad indeed.

What do *you* have to say about this? What is *your* analysis?

What does your next-door cricket expert tell you?

And yes, not to forget the passionate Indian cricket fan, with dreams in his eyes, may rubbish all of this saying that astrology is hogwash; Kohli and his team will power their way to victory and Dhoni will have a fairytale end.

Time will tell.

Prediction #3

Will India Beat Pakistan in the 2019 World Cup?

'I am not really bothered about India winning the 2019 World Cup. What I want to know is: will India beat Pakistan? If India defeats Pakistan, then the World Cup is won for me.' This would be most people's sentiments after the horrific Pulwama terror attack in February. The Indian team would want to bring some sort of solace to Indians by winning against the Pakistani team. Of course, all this will hold true if India actually agrees to play Pakistan in the 2019 World Cup.

In case the two teams do play, will India win the crucial match against Pakistan in the 2019 World Cup? The answer is a definite yes. The simple reason behind it is that Pakistan won a crucial match against India in 2017, the final of the Champions Trophy. That was one vital match in Sarfraz Ahmed's life—the biggest of them all—and by winning it he has lost the chance to beat India on an even bigger platform, which is the World Cup.

Sarfraz was born in 1987 and, by my calculation, Virat Kohli was born in 1986. So Virat has a better horoscope compared to Sarfraz. This time around the team Virat has is also better as compared to Pakistan's.

India is the favourite to win against Pakistan—and even astrology is with India.

So whether India wins the World Cup or not, the Indian fans can take heart from the fact that India's record against Pakistan in the World Cups will remain intact. It is possible that India can meet Pakistan twice in the tournament and if that happens, India will beat them the second time too.

Can India meet Pakistan in the finals of the World Cup 2019? Not possible at all. The chances of both or either of the teams winning the Cup are low and hence both will not meet in the final. What if they do meet? Then it is simple. Virat will win the World Cup as Sarfraz has already won the Champions League. However, that only remains a fantasy.

Prediction #4

Who Will be the 'Man-of-the-Match' in the 2019 World Cup Final?

4th February 2014. New Delhi.

I had always wondered what the exalted sun in the horoscope of the legendary cricketer, Sachin Tendulkar, meant. Sun indicates 'honour' and the tenth house indicates the government. People who occupy high offices in the government and/or are honoured by the government for some exceptional feat, always have the sun's connection to the tenth house or a powerful sun in their horoscopes. When Sachin was awarded the *Bharat Ratna,* the mystery was solved.

That brings us to another very important award while discussing World Cups: the Man-of-the-Match award. The cricketer who wins this award in a World Cup final is the one who had a decisive role in tilting the game in his country's favour. The more chances you have of that man being in your team, the better the chances of you winning the Cup. These are the men who take the bull by the horns and turn things around when their teams are facing adversity. Sometimes, they crush the opponents ruthlessly with an overpowering performance. They are the ones with the best horoscope amongst all.

These men-of-the-matches, too, come in patches. Let us look at these men since 1975:

Wasim Akram-Aravinda de Silva-Steve Waugh-Ricky Ponting-Adam Gilchrist-Mahendra Singh Dhoni-James Faulkner.

If you look at the birth years of these players you once again see an uncanny pattern in them: 1966-1965-1965-1974-1971-1981-1990.

If you notice, these are the years from the best patches. A 1977-born could not win a MOM as, astrologically, it was a slightly 'inferior' year compared to 1976 or 1978 or 1974 or 1981. Hence, during the 2011 WC final against India, when the 1977-born Mahela Jayawardene made a century and posted a challenging total against India, I didn't worry. I knew he wouldn't end up being the MOM. It had to be someone else. So, I had my hopes pinned on the openers, Sachin and Virender, who were born in 1973 and 1978 respectively, definitely better years than 1977. When both of them fell and Dhoni promoted himself in the order, it was very clear that a 1981 born—either Gambhir or Dhoni—would win the MOM.

The MOM's performance will always be match winning—or match saving when the entire team crumbles. He stands tall amidst all the ruin and salvages the situation by ensuring it wouldn't be a complete rout for them. While Mahendra Singh Dhoni gave a match-winning performance against Sri Lanka in 2011, Faulkner did the same against New Zealand for Australia in 2015. He killed the competition when he took the opposition's best batsman and captain, Brendon McCullum, in the very first over of the game. Match over. Another 1981-born, Michael Clarke, ensured that the match still was in Australia's favour, with a patient knock.

So, who will win the MOM in 2019 and win the match for his country? The clue to that comes from the sequence of the vital years. One important year that missed the sequence was 1986. It was a straight jump from 1981 to 1990. So, most probably the MOM will be a 1986–87-born. That is a greater reason why India shouldn't have Dhoni as their 'finisher'. It will be better to have a 1986–87 born in that slot. If we look at the Indian squad, we have only three players born in the years 1986–87: Ravichandran Ashwin, Suresh Raina and Rohit Sharma. There should be a 1986–87 born to finish the game for India, unless Rohit Sharma decides to a do a Ricky Ponting or Adam Gilchrist and helps India post a humongous score. So Suresh Raina fits the bill. Ashwin didn't appear in the playing XI that won the 2011 World Cup, though he had a good outing in some games. So, we can bet on him to produce a great spell too. Yes, we have three 1985-borns in India and they also have some chances to do that for you—Ambati Rayudu, Dinesh Karthik and Kedar Jadhav. But a team like England has 1986–87 born Eoin Morgan/ Moeen Ali as finishers, exactly the right age to have so.

There is also a possibility of a 1990-born winning the World Cup MoM in 2019 as the winning captain is going to be a 1986-born anyway. In that case, Jos Buttler and Joe Root loom large.

If we look at all the likely playing XI from the various countries, England have the maximum chances to win the MOM this time. They have about four 1986–87-born players and five-six players born in 1990. That is the biggest worry for India or any other country.

I have a feeling that the 1986-born Eoin Morgan is the one who could play that role other than Joe Root.

Morgan hasn't done anything phenomenal so far in his career despite his superb horoscope. How about winning the World Cup as a captain, for the first time ever, and playing a stupendous knock? Morgan has the sun in its own house. Well, Jos Buttler does too! You do need a very powerful sun to be feted with the highest awards of your country. Sachin Tendulkar became the *Bharat Ratna* because of the exalted sun in his tenth house (of career). If Morgan or Buttler are 'knighted', you know what that means, right?

Prediction #5

Can't Ravi Shastri's Horoscope Help India Win the World Cup?

June 2011. Mumbai.

'This is the horoscope of a CEO,' I said.

Vighnesh was perplexed. He was only interested in indulging in some fun conversation with me. Perhaps he didn't think I would seriously read his horoscope. 'Haha. No, I just wanted to know what you think my tenure here would be like.'

I replied, 'You are looking only at today. But, as an astrologer, I'm looking at tomorrow—or even three to five years down the line. Your horoscope is extremely powerful. You will go on to be a CEO. If not in this company, then in some other company. But it will happen for sure. And, yes, a very successful one at that.'

Vighnesh Shahane had Planet-X in the tenth house (of career), clearly indicating the topmost positions in life. He joined IDBI Federal Life Insurance Company as the head of Bancassurance. I was working in the Human Resources—Learning and Development function. Just a couple of months before he joined, my prediction in *DNA* that India would win the 2011 World Cup had come true and Vighnesh had come to know about that. Now, Vighnesh had an interesting story. The 1969-December-born was an ex-cricketer. He had played for the Mumbai Ranji team with the likes of Sachin Tendulkar, Sairaj Bahutule and Sanjay Bangar, to name a few. A freak accident left the six-feet-plus no option but to quit cricket, do his MBA and journey into the world of corporates.

On 20th March 2014, he became the CEO of IDBI Federal. He carried the passion of sports into business. With his intensity and drive he took the organisation from a ranking of about 16 to the top 10 in just five years.

Vighnesh had a fabulous horoscope. Only, he was destined to reach higher laurels as a CEO rather than as a cricketer. Sanjay Bangar was once just another cricketer, but he found his best career as a coach. Vighnesh's horoscope reminded me of another 1969-born, Shane Warne. Warne was a legend as a player, but his extraordinary horoscope also ensured that he won the inaugural IPL edition of the tournament as a coach. A coach also needs to have a good horoscope to win a big event like an IPL or a World Cup. Just like a CEO who motivates and propels his team to higher aspirations, a coach too does. A coach is the tail of the dinosaur who will win the World Cup. A strong tail ensures balance for the body and the head to function properly.

The coach is of supreme authority in football. He can make or break careers of footballers. He has the most unenviable job of selecting the right people who will perform for him and land the coveted trophy. The cricket coach doesn't enjoy that much control though. In fact, all the coaches who have tried to assert themselves have found themselves removed, especially in India. High-handedness of any kind is not tolerated by the players and they can even revolt against the coach, eventually leading them to be removed from the team. Ask Greg Chappel.

But teams that had incredible coaches, who had excellent people-management skills, not just survived but wrote extraordinary stories that turned into folklore. Ask Gary Kirsten.

Yes, there were some coaches whose ideology didn't match that of the captain and, eventually, they fell out. The coach in question here probably wanted certain things to be done in a certain way. The captain probably didn't like it; perhaps didn't want his authority diluted. In such a scenario the coach was even shown the door acrimoniously. Ask Anil Kumble.

Virat Kohli's handling of the Anil Kumble episode also emphasises the fact that he could not have been born in 1988. Had he been, he would have his sun and Mercury in Libra. Librans are known to always listen to different perspectives and then take decisions. Librans always end things amicably, even if there is a difference in the points of view. They are never into showdowns or getting into situations of 'You versus Me'. That is typically an Aries~Sagittarius~Scorpio trait, which could be the case if Virat was born in either 1986 or 1987.

I was unsure about Didier Deschamps' possibility of winning another huge title after already winning an UEFA Euro and WC as captain—especially with the 1960-born Argentine coach, Jorge Sampaoli, still in the fray. But when you looked deeper into Deschamps' timelines, he won the WC and the UEFA Euro in 1998 and 2000 when Pluto, Planet-X and Planet-Y were in strong positions, exactly the same planets that were in exaltation in his birth chart. Now there was one planet still to give him results and that was Uranus. An exalted Uranus was transiting his third house (of coaching) in 2018 and hence the karmic quota was accomplished now.

Coming back to the coaches, in cricket they may not be as powerful as those in football, but they do act as the yardstick from whom we can know if the team is going in the right direction. A coach with a great horoscope, appointed at a good time, would lead the team to great successes and vice versa.

Let us look at the likely scenarios during the upcoming 2019 World Cup to understand what may transpire.

The strongest coach for the 2019 World Cup is Justin Langer. Justin is already a World Cup-winner and a magnificent batsman. But look at his horoscope! The phenomenal Uranus, and Planet-Z definitely promise more. Had he been a World Cup-winning captain, I wouldn't have given him much importance. But he certainly still has some karmic quota of success up his sleeve. Justin Langer guarantees you at least one World Cup as a coach. So it is just a matter of finding out which World Cup Australia will win under him.

Mickey Arthur, the Pakistan coach, has already reaped the benefits of his horoscope by winning the Champions Trophy in 2017 against arch-rivals, India, besides taking Pakistan to the #1 ranked test and T20 team. So, another huge high for him seems improbable. South Africa has been making extraordinary blunders regarding the people at the helm. That's one of the reasons why they have never won a major ICC trophy or have the reputation of being 'chokers' who win all minor tournaments only to freeze in all the major ones at the most important stage. In Ottis Gibson they have an ordinary coach who will cap another ordinary World Cup year for the Proteas. Sad.

Trevor Bayliss, the 'tail' of England definitely has a marvellous horoscope. With deeply exalted Pluto and Neptune and other well-placed planets, England does have a major tournament-winning coach in him. In fact, he has already won a Big Bash League with Sydney Sixers, and two IPL tournaments with KKR as a coach. Can he still manage to win more? Yes, he can. He has not had an eventful career as a player and that works in his favour. He was born in the same year as Ravi Shastri and has almost the same planets as him if not better. What works in Trevor's favour is that unlike Shastri he doesn't have any impressive track record as a player. He hasn't utilised all his planets yet. His planets still have some magic left in them. With England, he may just turn on his biggest magic yet.

Ravi Shastri does have a good horoscope. However, his achievements are equally remarkable, at least looking at the potential of his horoscope. He is an accomplished all-rounder, the 'Champion of Champions' in the historic World Championship series in 1985, besides being an ace commentator. Immediately after he was appointed as a coach, I had written[1] how he would win great tournaments abroad if he ensures the right mix of personnel.

He had the best team in place while touring South Africa and England too in 2018. But glaring mistakes in selecting the players cost him the chances of winning two major tournaments outside the sub-continent. And then the final frontier was conquered. India won the test series for the first time in Australia after trying for more than 70 years in 2018–19. Team India became the

---

[1] Lobo, G. (2017, July 12). *Scientific astrologer says India will have successful overseas tours under Ravi Shastri*. Retrieved from: https://www.sportskeeda.com. Accessed on 17 February 2019.

sportskeeda

Scientific Astrologer says India will have successful overseas tours under Ravi Shastri

Greenstone Lobo FOLLOW
ANALYST

Feature
2.64K // 12 Jul. 2017

SHARE

Ravi Shastri was named the coach of the Indian team earlier this week

A quick glance at Ravi Shastri's horoscope without considering other factors like competition and team composition, yields a positive outlook for Team India.

first ever Asian team to defeat Australia at home. Ravi himself said[2] that this win was a greater victory for him than the 1983 World Cup win that he was a part of, though he didn't feature in the final match.

Well, if Ravi Shastri feels this is better than a World Cup win, then he may be right. He may never lead a team to a World Cup win, as he has already seen the best according to him. Well—all too good for his horoscope. Maybe there isn't anything further left now.

Ravi's acme of achievement would be done with once he steps down from being the coach of the Indian cricket team after the World Cup. Then it will all be about reflected glory. Ravi may never have another glorious career peak after this. He would, of course, continue to be an ace commentator. He could also find some additional success as an author, writer and columnist.

---

[2] Monga, S. (2019, January 07). *World cup winners Kohli and Shastri rate Australia win higher.* Retrieved from: http://www.espncricinfo.com. Accessed on 17 February 2019.

Prediction #6

Will RCB Win an IPL?

It is really surprising that Virat Kohli has not won an IPL yet. Yet it has been in India's greater interest. Virat has probably utilised all the energy of his karmic quota to win the overseas tests in South Africa and England in 2018 and some of those famous historic victories in Australia in 2019 he has accomplished so far.

Dhoni is a 1981-born and Rohit Sharma is a 1987-born and, of course, Virat Kohli was born in 1986 or 1987. The year 1981 was power-supreme. Between 2010 and 2018, both Dhoni and Rohit Sharma won the IPL thrice and Gautam Gambhir won it twice. The next few years are going to be ruled by the captains born in the years 1986–87, who will win the IPL. Therefore, it goes without saying that the time is in favour of Virat Kohli.

Virat will surely win an IPL for Royal Challengers Bangalore (RCB). It is on the cards and can happen anytime. It could even happen this year (2019). So while I am writing this, Virat's Royal Challengers Bangalore is one of the biggest challengers for the crown. If not this year, then it will happen sometime over the next two years. Virat is going to win an IPL; it is just a matter of time. If Virat Kohli doesn't win the World Cup 2019, then there are even greater chances that he will win an IPL soon. The vice versa, too, is true and in India's interest let's hope he doesn't win the IPL. RCB has a very good team in place and the man who was hindering the chances of the team, the *Amavasya*-born, Daniel Vettori, is no more their coach now and things will get better for them from here on.

The only factor which is still stopping Royal Challengers Bangalore from winning an IPL is, ironically, another coach. Gary Kirsten has done so much for cricket and won so many accolades that he probably has nothing left to win. This could probably be that one factor working against Virat. Let's hope that Gary has one last glory left to be gained and maybe that would translate into an IPL win. If Gary doesn't win it for them soon, then they would need to look for a new coach. RCB have the best captain and probably the best team in place. The only non-working factor right now is the coach. Sometimes, having the best man in place for a purpose may not be the best idea.

Prediction #7
Which Captains Will Win the Future IPLs?

The horoscope of the captain is the key in winning mega tournaments such as an IPL. As we have seen in the past, only the best players with the best horoscopes can win the IPL. In the last 11 years (as of 2018), the captains who have won the cash-rich event were born in the years 1969, 1971, 1981, 1986 and 1987, with the 1981- and 1987-borns winning it thrice! As we have discussed a few times in the book, the 1986–87 phenomenon is going to work for the IPL in the future too. The year 1985 is also very important and cannot be discounted. So Dinesh Karthik, the only 1985-born captain, will always be on the radar.

The year which follows the 1986–87 belt is 1990. The year 1990 will be followed by the years 1992–94. So the IPL-winning captains of the future look like this: the 1987-born Rohit Sharma will always be in the reckoning as he has the finest horoscope amongst all the captains. Besides, he has not been captaining India regularly, so he has some karmic quota still intact. Therefore, he is the most important captain to watch out for. The 1986-born Virat Kohli and Ravichandran Ashwin will always be dangerous and both should win at least one IPL each.

If any other major player born in the stretch of 1986–87, like Suresh Raina, Kieron Pollard, Aaron Finch,

Shakib Al-Hasan or Chris Morris, is made the captain, then they too have chances to win the IPL.

One of the biggest players who has a great chance to win an IPL is captain Kane Williamson, a 1990-born. His chances are higher as there is little possibility of him winning a World Cup or a similiar event as the captain of the New Zealand team.

I am really surprised that the test captain of the English team, Joe Root, is not playing in the IPL. If some smart franchise can make him their captain, he should certainly win an IPL. Branding Root as a test player is premature. He can surprise most with his scores in the shortest format of the game as well.

Jos Butler, too, could be one dangerous and lucky captain. Kane, Jos and Joe were all born in the year 1990.

The next lot of captains could be born in 1992–94. We can see some real gems here in Quinton de-Kock, Hardik Pandya, Sanju Samson, Kuldeep Yadav, KL Rahul and Shivam Dube. Shivam will be playing his first IPL when this book goes to print, but I'm pretty excited about the potential of his horoscope.

It is always possible that some players, whose names are not mentioned here, might win the IPL tournament as captain. But they would invariably be born in those strategic years—1986, 1987, 1990, 1992, 1993 and 1994 in the next few editions. By the time those born in the 1990s get into action, the scene would have changed for the coaches too. The coaches born during the years 1968–74 would have higher chances now to win an IPL, combining forces with a captain born in the 1990s. The 1980–82-born coaches would come next in forming the fantastic IPL-winning teams.

Prediction #8

What are India's Chances in the 2020 ICC World T20?

When our school mates decided to meet after 20 years, I was surprised to hear some of my classmates asking if 'athlete' Greenstone was coming for the get-together. I remember faintly that I used to sprint well and even was an above-average footballer during my schooldays. But, I never played cricket. One sport which I loved to play was kabaddi. I used to be the 'raider' who would 'visit' the opposing team in their den. Making a 'super raid', touching two or three opponents and escaping away to safety was a daredevilry that raised my adrenaline levels. Boy, did I love it! I found cricket very long, dull and boring and never played it. Funnily enough, I have written volumes on cricket and nothing on kabaddi!

The T20 World Cup in 2020 will be played in Australia. Strangely, the winner of this World Cup will remain a champion for only a year. The next year, in 2021, there will be another T20 World Cup. That is the ICC's strange way of scheduling a tournament!

So, what are the chances that India can win the Cup in 2020?

It is never easy to predict a tournament's result so much in advance, since the horoscopes of the captains, the coaches and the team members play a big role in deciding it. The teams are yet to be known. But what we could try and do, on the basis of Virat's horoscope alone, is hazard an educated guess about the possibilities from India's perspective.

The 2019 win would have given one 1986-born captain a win, that is Eoin Morgan or Aaron Finch. I assume it would be Morgan as we have mentioned several times before. There is a miniscule chance that Aaron Finch will win it instead. In either case, there are two other 1986-born great players around, who also need to have equal chances to win a World Cup. They are the two captains out of the trio of Eoin Morgan, Virat Kohli and Aaron Finch, except whoever wins the Cup in 2019. They both need to win a World Cup each. Or at least one of them *has* to win a World Cup. But, since the tournament will be played in Australia, the chances of Australia winning grow higher, especially if they don't win the 2019 event.

Can a 1990-born win a World Cup now? As mentioned before, 1990 is the next best year in the queue after the patch of 1986–87. But, a win now is not possible at all. The 1990-borns will be able to win huge tournaments only after 2021, when Pluto gets exalted. So, New Zealand captain Kane Williamson has no chances this time.

India's chances of winning the 2020 T20 World Cup brighten, especially as they would have some deadwood removed from their team by then—and will also have a new coach as Ravi Shastri will step down after the 2019 World Cup. India would then have a fairly good chance, with a new set of young players. But they will still face competition from either Australia or England, depending on which one of them does not win the Cup in 2019.

In scenario #1, assuming England wins the 2019 World Cup:

England has already won a cup under Eoin Morgan and cannot repeat the feat again. The greatest chance of winning the T20 World Cup in Australia in 2020 goes to Australia. Aaron Finch—born on a full-moon day—has the best chance to win it in his own den. Australia's chances also grow significantly because now they also have a terrific coach in Justin Langer. Langer's horoscope says he has to win a World Cup. So, India's chances grow rather thin here.

India may have a chance—*if* they rid themselves of the non-performing assets in their team or replace their old warriors with new ones. We will discuss the possible winning team in a chapter to follow. India's chances would also brighten under a new coach. Hopefully, the birth year of the new coach will fall between 1965 and 1975 and he will have good planets in the right houses.

In scenario #2, assuming Australia wins the 2019 World Cup:

The best chances to win the 2020 World Cup then go to England. Eoin Morgan doesn't play tests and the only glory he can achieve is in the ODIs or the T20 World Cup or the IPL. As none of the IPL teams will make him the captain, he should be the best man to win the World Cup in 2020. The extraordinary team under Morgan hasn't won a big tournament yet and it will win it this time.

India has the second best chance to win the 2020 World Cup since Virat has a spectacular horoscope. If he has a great squad, then, as a 1986-born, he will undoubtedly have great chances to win the World.

Australia still has a chance to win the T20 World Cup in 2020 even if it wins the 2019 event. This man, Aaron Finch, has an extra-special horoscope. It seems he is destined to win a World Cup. Will it be two? A 50-over one as well as a 20-over one? Well, he does have the potential to accomplish that feat! So, Australia will be the super-favourite to win this tournament.

So, the highest chances to win the T20 World Cup in 2020 go to:

1. Australia
2. India
3. England

I'm not talking about the possibility of any other team at all as none of them stands a chance. That includes Pakistan, Sri Lanka, Bangladesh and South Africa.

Well, Indian fans need to cheer up. There is a great chance here, especially if we don't win the 2019 event.

Talking of T-Rex, both Australia and India would have a fantastic head, body and tail and hence almost equal chances. As the Australian T-Rex's head isn't as celebrated as the Indian T-Rex's, I would consider it to have a slight edge over us. But we can cling on to the hope that the Indian T-Rex would still emerge stronger and victorious—and hopefully do a successful 'super-raid' on the Aussies, I hope. And hope is a good thing.

The only problem with this is that Virat has already created history through a 'super raid' in Australia by leading India to victory for the first time on Australian soil in a test series in 2018–19. Would he be able to do something similar again? Well, it is anyone's guess. I had anticipated this dilemma (both the WC and the historic test series win highly unlikely on Australian soil) and hence predicted[1] that Virat would win a maiden test series in Australia. Between winning a test series Down Under and a World Cup Down Under, the first one seemed more probable, especially as there was a weak captain in the 1984-born Tim Paine. But in the 2020 World Cup, the Aussie captain would be the 1986-born Aaron Finch and it would be a tough job to do it once again. Lightning never strikes the same place twice.

---

[1] Lobo, G. (2018, December 08). *India vs Australia: Will Virat Kohli create history down under? Astrologer Greenstone Lobo predicts*. Retrieved from: https://www.dnaindia.com. Accessed on 17 February 2019.

Prediction #9

Can Smith and Warner Stop India from Winning in Australia Again?

India's historic win in Australia for the first time ever in a test series occurred in 2018–19. Many people feel that the case would have been different had Steven Smith and David Warner been a part of the Australian team.

Is that so? Also, what will happen when India goes to Australia again and faces a team that does have Steve Smith and David Warner? Can these two players stop India from winning on its home soil again?

Let's get this right. India won the test series in Australia because of one reason alone—that the captain of the Australian team was Tim Paine. Poor chap was born in 1984 on a full-moon day. 'Poor' because he captained the weakest team in terms of performance. The full moon made him the captain. Unfortunately for him, he was against Virat Kohli, who has one of the best horoscopes ever. Tim Paine was born for this painful moment for Australia—to captain them at their lowest point. Unfortunately, he was the chosen one. Just how good is Paine's horoscope? Well, as good as Murali Vijay's, who is another 1984, full-moon born.

Virat hasn't won a World Cup so far. He was supposed to have some extraordinary wins under his belt and that is why he won in Australia for the first time. So, in a scenario where Tim Paine is the captain once again, even if Steven Smith plays under him, then India under Virat Kohli will beat Australia once again. But that is highly unlikely since Tim Paine will never be the captain again.

Now when India visits Australia again, it will be a different story. Who would be the captain? In all probability, Steven Smith, but it could also be someone else too, maybe even Aaron Finch. Steven Smith will not win the World Cup since he will not be the captain of the limited-over teams. That means he will be able to fulfil his karmic quota of success only in the test matches. That makes him really dangerous and his chances of winning against any other team become much more powerful.

Aaron Smith has a good horoscope anyway, probably as good as Kohli's. When a player with a 'not-so-good' horoscope captains a team, the best arsenal of the team fails to fire, simply because if he does, then his team will win, which was not supposed to happen. That was exactly what happened when India won the historic test series in Austrlia in 2018–19. Aaron just didn't fire. If Aaron becomes the captain himself, he will find his mojo back and can be a hugely dangerous player that we all know he is.

So, the next time India visits Australia, there is a very little chance that they will pull off a spectacular victory once again in a test series, especially if Tim Paine is not the captain.

Prediction #10

Will India Ever Win a Test Series in South Africa?

India have never won a test series in South Africa. They have been trying since 1992, but could never cross the line. The maximum they could achieve was a draw. Everyone from Mohammad Azharuddin, Sourav Ganguly, Rahul Dravid, MS Dhoni and Virat Kohli have failed. I wondered why.

It may sound absurd, but the reason why Indians could never win a series in South Africa is because South Africa never won the ICC tournaments! The captains retained their karmic quota of success by not winning any major tournaments. So, they won everything else. No wonder SA won almost every bilateral series. Everyone has to win something and the South African captains won the tournaments at home. Hence, another team would only have a chance to win a test series against South Africa in South Africa if their captain wins a World Cup. But that doesn't seem to be possible anytime soon.

Also, it has to be mentioned that historically, starting from Kepler Wessels, the South African captains have had really strong horoscopes. But they just fell short of the best by a whisker and that's the reason they couldn't win any ICC tournaments. Only Hansie Cronje won an ICC trophy, but there was a tragic end to his career and then to his life due to other planets.

The current South African test captain is Dean Elgar. Now this man has a fantastic horoscope. He was also born in 1987 and on a full-moon day, which makes him a potential icon of the game. It is ironical that he is not playing the ODIs when South Africa have a potential World Cup winner in their midst. I shudder to think of the possibilities South Africa might have if Dean Elgar were their ODI captain. Thankfully for the other countries, he is not.

It is sad that some players are branded as test or T20 players, when they actually have the capacity to achieve something even bigger. Dean Elgar is one of them. That means if Dean Elgar is still the captain of the test team, it will be very difficult for the other teams to beat South Africa, unless they have a really extraordinary captain themselves.

Virat Kohli has achieved much in life. In comparison, Dean Elgar has not achieved anything extraordinary. This may work against India and especially Virat, who will not be able to win a test series in South Africa in such a scenario. Maybe in the third attempt? Maybe. Or perhaps if he doesn't win a World Cup at all. Can India perform a miracle as Sri Lanka did in February 2019 in Durban? Kusal Perera played an epic knock to steal a last wicket win against the Faf Du Plessis-led South African team in their home soil. I doubt if Sri Lanka would have pulled off that spectacular win if Elgar was the captain. India's chances definitely brighten up in the next couple of test series in South Africa if Faf Du Plessis remains their captain.

Prediction #11

What are India's Chances in the 2021 ICC World T20?

'Greenie, you need a story. Create a story around yourself. A story sells. We need something fancier than just a Christian boy with no background or upbringing in astrology, who goes on to be a good astrologer. If required, invent something!' The social media consultant exclaimed with exaggerated hand movements.

So, here I was requesting a humble flyer created on Photoshop and he was selling his services as a consultant. In hindsight, what he said made a lot of sense. Everyone loves a hero who wins against all odds and extreme circumstances. It is appalling how the media can sometimes exaggerate stories just so that we have something interesting to read/watch.

But Virat's could be a real-life hero story if he has never won a World Cup before and goes on to win the 2021 edition. Just like it happened for Pakistan's Imran Khan in 1992. Winning the World Cup at 40, in your last competitive match! What a dream end!

Would Virat have such a story? Going against the odds and winning it when everyone is writing you off as a captain who stumbles when it comes to winning ICC tournaments?

This World Cup will be played in India and India will, naturally, be the favourites to win the tournament. Let's examine the astrological chances for India in various scenarios:

1. If India has won the 2020 World Cup (The basic assumption is that it has not won the 2019 World Cup): In this case, it will become difficult for India to win any World Cup under Virat Kohli again. If Virat has already won a World Cup in 2020, then he will have no choice but to give way to either of the other two guys to win the next World Cup.

   The composition of the team or the coach will not matter then. The captaincy of Finch or Morgan will be enough to win the World Cup. In fact, in this World Cup, there is an additional danger for India in the form of Sri Lanka. Remember, Angelo Mathews, too, is a 1987-born. Though Mathews hasn't been on the right side of the selectors of late, but there is always a chance that he may come back as the captain. If he does, then the Lankans have some chances as well.

   Sri Lanka's incredible crop of young players was born around the 1993 period, making them deadly dangerous. Sri Lanka may return to their heyday under their coach, Hathurasinghe, and captain, Mathews. Do not forget that cricket-wise, Sri Lankans would love the sub-continent pitches on offer in India. They wouldn't be alien as the Lankan players play in the IPL too. Even if the Lankans are captained by Dinesh Chandimal, they still have good chances.

So, not just Australia and England, but even Sri Lanka could win this World Cup if Virat Kohli has the 2020 World Cup in his kitty. Bangladesh is one team that doesn't seem to be throwing up good captains or players. Their players are just above average. Hope some future Bangladeshi player emerges stronger. We need to keep a watch on both Bangladesh and Afghanistan. As of now, both the countries seem good, but just not good enough.

2. If India has not won a World Cup under Virat Kohli so far: This will be a great chance for Virat Kohli to win a World Cup for India. England would have won under Eoin in England in 2019; Australia would have won it in Australia in 2020 and India will do exactly the same in 2021. The World Cup happening in India under all too familiar conditions will add to the possibilities. If India has never won a World Cup under Virat before, then this will be their best chance. For Virat it will be a case of now or never.

   All three 1986-born captains winning a World Cup each will happen now.

3. This World Cup will also go only to a 1986-born. Remember, this World Cup will be played for the last time before Pluto enters the zodiac sign Capricorn in 2021. Once Pluto enters Capricorn, it will become extremely difficult for a 1986–87-born to win large tournaments any further. This is the final instalment when the 1986–87-borns can rule the roost.

Here are three contenders for this:

Australia could always win it once again under Aaron. He has a birth chart that can give him back-to-back T20 World Cups. The fact that all the Australian players play in the IPL every year anyway, makes them more comfortable with the conditions here. So, don't be surprised if they go on to win yet another tournament. They have the captain and the team to do it.

The only other possibility is that India would have won in Australia in 2020 against all odds and Aaron Finch would extract revenge by winning it in India. While India keeps the World Cup for a year, Australia would for a longer time.

The team that looks capable of surprising everyone is the Sri Lankan team. They will be at their best at this time. Sri Lanka poses the biggest threat this time around to Virat's India. Virat can win this World Cup only if there is a huge overhauling in the Indian team. Also, Virat's chances will go up only if there is a good coach for India this time round. If Virat has never won a World Cup before, then this will also prove to be his last and best chance to win it.

So, the teams with the best chances to win the 2021 World Cup will be:

1. India
2. Australia
3. Sri Lanka
4. England

This, of course, is based on the various assumptions, ifs and buts, and a lot of terms and conditions as discussed earlier.

We cannot do a T-Rex comparison here as we are not sure of the players and the coaches. But it suffices to know that India has some great chances to win this World Cup.

If Virat indeed was born in 1986–87, then he *has to* win a World Cup and it seems this would be that time. A fab new team under Virat winning at home. That would complete an astonishing run of three teams winning World Cups in their backyard—England in 2019, Australia in 2020 and India in 2021.

If Virat hasn't won a World Cup as a captain until 2021, there is very little chance that he will later. There would probably be no great story in the making. Nor would there be folklore. You need the planet, Pluto, in place to create folklore. Imran Khan had it; so did Kapil Dev. And, indeed, Arjuna Ranatunga. Virat Kohli doesn't. There lies the difference.

Prediction #12

What Could Be the Indian XI That Can Win a World Cup?

Alright, so this is one prediction that can spark of a lot of debate. We Indians love discussing who we would like to see in the playing 11 of the Indian cricket team.

Now, here is my team that can potentially win a World Cup. I have given two or three names for certain spots, but mentioned just one for some. So, it's about a pool of 15 cricketers from where the playing 11 can be selected.

The logic behind the selection is simple: the men with the best horoscopes will play for the country. The men born in the best years and at the best of times will be in the playing 11. This also includes the players who are of the right age. I have taken care to ensure that these are the players who have the potential to win a World Cup in their horoscopes but, at the same time, haven't completed their karmic quota of success.

The patch of greatness which comes after 1990 is 1992–1994, 1997 and beyond. The majority of the players should be born in 1993. The captain, being the most important person, should have the best horoscope amongst all. As of now, we don't have any player who has a better horoscope than Virat Kohli. So here are the best 11 who can win the World Cup for India.

We need to remember that the opposition can still come up with a stronger team than ours but this, according to my astrological calculations is our best team going forward for the next two T20 World Cups to be played in Australia and India in the years 2020 and 2021 respectively.

(1987) Rohit Sharma

(1992) KL Rahul

(1986) Virat Kohli (Captain)

(1994) Shreyas Iyer

(1990) Suryakumar Yadav/ Sarfaraz Khan (1997)/ Shivam Dube (1993)

(1993) Hardik Pandya

(1997) Rishabh Pant (WK)

(1994) Kuldeep Yadav/ Mayank Markhande (1997)

(1993) Jasprit Bumrah

(1990) Yuzvendra Chahal/ or a fast bowler born in the years 1993–98

(1990) Mohd Shami/ Khaleel Ahmed (1997)

This team would have a 1986 born captain, a 1987 born vice-captain (Rohit Sharma), two-three players born in 1990, one player born in 1992, at least two players born in 1993, two players born in 1994 and at least two players born in 1997—an almost perfect recipe to win a World Cup, astrologically. Unless other teams outthink us, of course.

Some of the top/better known players have not made this squad, as they are either overage and cannot be considered or have completed their quota of success or have karmic quota elsewhere. On the other hand, some may be too young to win a World Cup right now.

Prediction #13

Who Will Be the Future Ranji Trophy-Winning Captains?

'All the world's a stage, and all the men and women merely players,' said William Shakespeare. Talking about the stage and films, the actors and performers with the best horoscopes win Oscars and Grammys. In India it could be the National Award or the Filmfare or some regional ones or relatively less-known awards which not many would notice. The interesting bit is that we all play our part depending upon the horoscope we have got.

In sports, players with the best horoscopes win Olympic medals, the FIFA World Cup or the ICC World Cup. Players with slightly 'lesser' horoscopes would win the IPL or major club championships and those with even less remarkable horoscopes would win a Ranji Trophy.

I don't intend to demean the Ranji Trophy in any way (that is not my intention at all), but I do need to mention that, ironically, it is amongst the lowest in the hierarchy of achievements in cricket.

The captains who win the Ranji Trophy normally have less significant horoscopes compared to captains who win the IPL or the World Cups. So, you will notice that the captain who has won the Ranji Trophy was probably born in the years that haven't been discussed as important years astrologically.

The last Ranji Trophy in 2018 and 2019 was won by Vidarbha and the captain was Faiz Fazl—born in 1985. Parthiv Patel, another 1985-born, won the Ranji Trophy in 2017. Aditya Tare, who was born at the fag end of 1987, won it for Mumbai in 2016. Vinay Kumar, a 1984-born, won it for Karnataka in 2014 and 2015. Ajit Agarkar, a 1977-born, won it for Mumbai in 2013.

So the pattern we see here is that the captains in particular years, who had the best planets at that time, but not as good as those in the best years, were chosen to be the winners of the Ranji Trophy. For example, the years 1986 and 1987 are amongst the strongest years astrologically. However, none of the recent Ranji Trophy-winning captains were born at that time. This proves how astrology works.

In future, too, we will see that Ranji Trophy-winning captains would be born in such astrologically weaker years—all the years that may not be the greatest in terms of astrological significance, but still have some spark in them. Some of such future years would be 1988, 1989, 1991 and 1992. Dinesh Karthik, a 1985-born captain, could certainly win the title for Tamil Nadu if he doesn't win the IPL for KKR. Ajinkya Rahane, a 1988-born, could win it for Mumbai, and a similar feat could be achieved by the 1988-born Cheteshwar Pujara or Ravindra Jadeja for Gujarat. Karun Nair of 1991, Umesh Yadav of late-1987, Dhawal Kulkarni of 1988, Jaydev Unadkat of 1991, Krunal Pandya of 1991, Siddhesh Lad of 1992, Shikhar Dhawan of 1985, Ishant Sharma of 1988, Manish Pandey of 1989, Vijay Shankar of 1991 are potential Ranji Trophy winning-captains. There could even be some Ranji Trophy legends born in those strategic years but never known in the circuits outside, like Faiz Fazl, who was not known to many until he led Vidarbha to Ranji trophy victory in 2018.

Prediction #14

What Now for Anil Kumble?

Lots of drama unfolded after Anil Kumble became the head coach of the Indian cricket team in 2016. Much before the end of his tenure he fell out with the captain, Virat Kohli, and had to relinquish his position unceremoniously. Ravi Shastri took over after that and India went on to achieve many milestone victories, especially while touring abroad.

Shastri is all set to step down from his post after the World Cup in 2019. Everyone knows that Anil Kumble will still not get an opportunity to coach India again because he is not in the good books of the Indian captain—the man who matters the most. It seems that at least temporarily Kumble is out of the reckoning for any top position with the BCCI. But, let me assure you, for Kumble everything is not over yet.

Pluto will be moving into Anil's third house in 2021 and will stay there until 2039. This is a very interesting house. The third house indicates the brain, the tongue and the hands. If you try to interpret this, it means that he may have a strategic or a thinking role or do something significant using his hands. It is also an indicator of teaching, training, coaching and writing. As far the role of the hands is concerned, diehard cricket fans may remember that Kumble is a huge photography enthusiast. He may just take his passion for photography to the next level.

What else could this planetary movement translate into for him? I wouldn't be surprised if he is already into some kind of writing, maybe even preparing some kind of coaching manual. He may land up as some type of an analyst, a performance coach or assume a role which would require a lot of communication. Pluto will bring him back in the reckoning once again.

Major planetary transits to the third house made Zinedine Zidane and Didier Deschamps achieve their greatest successes as coaches during 2015–18. Kumble too should be back for some form of coaching. If he doesn't coach the Indian cricket team, he may do it for some other cricket team. He hasn't been the head coach of any IPL team and he may just become one.

Virat Kohli is a Scorpio. There's little possibility that he would forget the altercation he had with Kumble. So Kumble's chances to work with the national cricket team in any capacity will surface only after Kohli ceases to be the captain. Let us hope that he manages to do something for India because he can certainly be a very good and successful coach. As Pluto stays for a longer term, Kumble could do it even after Virat leaves the scene. Yes, Jumbo does have an important and interesting unwritten chapter in his life, which will unfold post-2021.

Prediction #15

What Now for Sourav Ganguly?

Sourav Ganguly had a superb career as a batsman—one of the greatest in ODI cricket. He is not done yet. His second innings will be bigger and brighter and, of course, less riddled with controversies.

Jupiter, which is very powerfully placed in Dada's chart, could make him shine in the Indian literary firmament. Yes, he is in the editing panel of *Wisden* and has also recently released his autobiography. But there is probably more to it than meets the eye. Ganguly can be a very good teacher, guru and a mentor. A strong Jupiter also makes one a good leader of men, which he was as a captain. It remains to be seen if he will exercise that Jupiterian option now and if he does, how it will benefit Indian cricket. He had a spat with a former coach and probably realises what should go into coaching.

Ganguly took Indian cricket to new levels. He created match winners in the team. He made India a fighting unit. All the famous victories in the recent years can perhaps be traced back to the Ganguly days where they saw their genesis. Individually, he was one of the greatest scorers in ODI cricket.

Dada too is not done yet. Another feather remains to be added to the Prince of Kolkata's crown. Dada can even become the Dada of Indian cricket. He is already the president of the Cricket Association of Bengal (CAB) but that is a relatively low position, considering the planets in his chart. The transiting Uranus could take him to another level altogether. Uranus will be in Sourav's first house of personality till 2024. During this time his stature as a person is bound to grow. He could go to the next level. From being the president of the Bengal Cricket Association he could become the president of the BCCI. This position would offer him greater glory. India could shine even brighter if it happens.

Prediction #16

What Now for Sachin Tendulkar?

Arguably the greatest batsman ever to have walked on the planet, Sachin Tendulkar spent a quarter of a century playing international cricket and scored a hundred international centuries. He is the highest scorer of all time with a record of the highest number of runs in tests and ODIs and remains one of the richest sportspersons in the world—and a *Bharat Ratna* awardee at 40!

What more can someone achieve? Hasn't Sachin achieved everything a person can hope for? Is there something still left in his wishlist? What could that be?

A closer look at the Little Master's horoscope shows two areas in his life where he can still achieve something significant. Some unfinished business lingers but one of those is definitely not politics! He will rise above politics and do something even more radical and meaningful than he can ever hope to as a politician.

Planet-Z will enter his second house of wealth and the fourth house of luxury, property and homeland between 2026 and 2048. The first area where Sachin could do phenomenally well is business. No, I am not saying that he will become a boardroom master—far from it! Sachin doesn't exactly have a business mind.

Being an Aries-Sagittarius-Pisces, he is passionate, full of positivity and has the mind of a monk. He is the quintessential sportsperson. He can never be tarnished by the big bad world of business. But he might lend his name to some good business deals that will be fruitful, some associations which will benefit by his presence; he might make some smart moves that will bring in huge dividends. Most of them will be connected with sports and entertainment.

The biggest change Sachin Tendulkar will be involved in will be *social*. Pluto will be exalted in his seventh house from 2021 to 2038. This will be a period when he will make some significant contributions to society. He may be instrumental in bringing in great changes in certain aspects of the society. His impact will be large and radical. He may just start a movement of sorts, though not political. He will impact the physical well-being and improve conditions of thousands of people. He will do his best to make the world a better place. The society has given him a lot; he will give back to the society in a big way. He will be a catalyst for some significant change.

Prediction #17

What Now for Virender Sehwag?

A person's horoscope indicates various events that will unfold over their lifetime. Some people have planets arranged in a way that shows their main career to be only a minor story, but there may be many other things going on around that career. For instance, a doctor by education and profession could choose to work in someone else's hospital, set up his own practice, be a speaker, open a cafe as a side business or even stand for elections. There would be various planets in their horoscope, which throw up all these possibilities.

When you look at Sachin Tendulkar's horoscope, or Sourav Ganguly's, Rahul Dravid's or even Anil Kumble's, you will notice that they have not exhausted all the possibilities yet. Ravi Shastri is one person who has utilised about 50 percent of the power of his planets as a cricket player for India. He went on to add more feathers to his cap even after he stopped playing. Sunil Gavaskar and Dilip Vengsarkar also had such ratios. Besides being exceptional players with good achievements, these gentlemen also had great careers post retirement.

When I look at the horoscope of Virender Sehwag, I wonder if he squeezed out everything possible while he was still a player. Sehwag has Jupiter, Chiron,

Planet-X and Planet-Y in exalted positions. These planets have made him, if you can use the word, a cricket 'great'. He happens to be one of the greatest openers India has ever produced. Besides, he is also a World Cup winner. But by being that great player Sehwag has used up almost all the possibilities of all the planets. I would say that probably just Planet-Y may have some minor impact upon his career ahead. Sehwag can be a funny commentator and a part-time columnist besides entertaining people with his witty tweets. He may continue with these and never really have another great alternative career. So, he may not end up as a great administrator or a fantastic coach. He would just reap the rewards from being a great ex-player.

If Sehwag is reading this, he would probably shrug his shoulders in his nonchalant style and say, 'So how does that matter?' Yes, actually, it doesn't matter. Not for Sehwag. He has done enough already. It is time now for him to enjoy himself and bask in that huge legacy he has created.

Prediction #18

What Now for Yuvraj Singh?

Yuvraj Singh was born exactly when the planet Uranus reached its exaltation point after 84 years. He has a phenomenal horoscope. Going by the events in his life, astrologically, he cannot be a 1981-born. The year 1979 looks more likely. This year also shows how he emerged as one of the greatest cricketers ever from India and why he still had to suffer through cancer.

Yuvraj has done what no Indian cricketer has done so far. He has played in three World Cup wins for India—the Under-19 World Cup, the 50-overs World Cup and the T20 World Cup! That is legendary. Be it his six sixes in an over, those umpteen chasing of targets or the man-of-the-tournament performance in the 2011 World Cup—he has been there and done it all.

Yuvraj Singh has such a great track record of coming back when people write him off, that people expect him to do miracles. Some people expect him to come back even now. He is definitely not in the scheme of things for World Cup 2019, but some of his loyal fans are still dreaming that he would have another great win up his sleeve, maybe even a wild-card entry into the World Cup in England. Perhaps, maybe an IPL win. Well, all of these may not materialise in reality.

Yuvraj is trying to reverse the clock, but will not be able to succeed. After 2019 he will have no choices as, over the next couple of years, Planet-X and Planet-Z will be transiting into challenging houses for him. Yuvraj will continue to inspire millions with YouWeCan and other such initiatives. But his career as a sports person is almost over.

Another thing that needs to be mentioned here is that Yuvraj, too, like his contemporary Virender Sehwag, has squeezed out most of the karmic quota of his life—both good and bad. He will fail miserably if he tries to make it as a coach or as an entrepreneur.

During his playing career he has always been a number two; never a number one (a captain or a leader). His stints as a leader ended in failure like in the IPL. Even in the future Yuvi's successes will only come as a number two. He could collaborate with some strong partners in his business ventures. Going solo wouldn't be a good idea. Yuvraj needs to be very careful about his future investments or he may end up making grave mistakes.

Prediction #19

Dhoni for Chief Minister of Jharkhand?

An interesting idea has been floating around in the country for a while—that MS Dhoni will one day become the Chief Minister of Jharkhand. I'm not sure whose fantasy it is but, if that happens, it will be really big, isn't it? Is there really a possibility of that happening? Let's examine his chart.

We have dissected Dhoni's horoscope threadbare in the earlier chapters. As you know by now, MSD has exploited most of the possibilities of his fantastic planets. Uranus made him a great batsman, who pulled India out of the woods many a time even until recently. Planet-Y made him a calculating, shrewd captain. Both these planets have also given him two cricket World Cups. The one planet whose impact Dhoni has not extracted so far is Chiron. Chiron is Dhoni's second lord exalted in the eleventh house. This might make him a great businessman in the later part of his life. So, one of the biggest possibilities for Dhoni post-retirement would be as a successful businessman.

Is there a possibility that he can be elevated to a high position in the public sphere or in the government? Yes, that's quite possible. He could even be a minister, perhaps the minister of sports. He could be appointed in certain positions like Sachin. Sachin Tendulkar became an MP in the Rajya Sabha through the agency of government personnel. Dhoni could also find himself similarly appointed.

For someone to become a Chief Minister they need to win elections. That requires a very powerful seventh house. Dhoni doesn't have any planet exalted in his seventh house. He is a leader for sure, but he is a leader in sports and not politics. Expecting him to become the Chief Minister of a state would be stretching it a bit too far.

Is there a possibility of a party making him the head of state after they win the elections? In that case, Dhoni would need to have a strong tenth house like Manmohan Singh had and he doesn't have that either. Well, that too seems too much of wishful thinking than an actual possibility.

But does Dhoni really need that? He doesn't. He will do well in his business and continue being an influential figure in Indian sports for a long time. Meanwhile, don't be surprised if some fans in Tamil Nadu try to build a temple for their '*thalaiva*'. That seems a distinct possibility.

Prediction #20

What is the Future of Gautam Gambhir?

Gautam Gambhir is probably one of the most unfortunate players in Indian cricket, who didn't receive the kind of admiration and recognition he richly deserved. Being the highest scorer in both the recent World Cup wins is testimony enough to the nerves of steel that the man possesses. The significance of those wonderful knocks is evident from the fact that he played them when the chips were down.

Gautam's horoscope very clearly shows that he would go through extreme mental and emotional turmoil in his career. Hopefully, retired now, he can be less *gambhir* in future as he won't be competing with anyone anymore and the fierce competitor in him can relax.

Gautam does have it in him to be successful as a coach. He can do it straightaway. He may find immediate success, too. Uranus is transiting his ninth house of teaching and this could be the best time for him to coach or even write a book maybe. He could be the coach of an IPL team too. Besides, he could be a commentator too. Being as outspoken as he is, his comments could sometimes rake up a few controversies. He won't be a yes man, you see. Gautam will continue to be the forthright person he has always been.

Gautam will do something really substantial for the political landscape of the country. His leadership may well be visible in the political circles. He does want to contribute his bit to his country and he will do a great job of it. Just like Dhoni, he won't be a leader elected to the topmost position but secondary ones are definitely possible. His fiery speeches could play a good role too. Gautam will also make some sensible business decisions. An exalted Chiron in his eleventh house indicates that the second half of his life will be happier and more successful, especially as a businessman. He didn't get his due as a sportsperson, but he will undoubtedly get his due as a politician and as a businessman.

Gautam always lost out to MS Dhoni on the cricket field despite being an excellent achiever. Luck didn't favour him because Pluto was weakly placed in his fifth house of recognition, which robbed him of some of the glory. But it is a level playing field now. Gambhir and Dhoni are equals now. Both of them will reach almost equal positions in their career connected to politics. Monetarily and business-wise, Dhoni may be slightly ahead. But otherwise they will be equals.

Prediction #21

What Will Happen to Mithali Raj?

Mithali Raj missed greatness by a whisker—relatively speaking, that is. The 1982-born was unlucky that she didn't have a fantastic team except for a couple of good players. She couldn't become the male equivalent of MS Dhoni despite being born a few months apart from him. She is probably one of the greatest women players of all time, but she could have done better. Yes, she is the female superstar of Indian cricket and was responsible for bringing the spotlight on women's cricket but, given the planets she has, she could have achieved more.

Now that she is at the fag end of her career, it may not be possible for her to do something phenomenal. She came very close to winning the World Cup in 2005 and then in 2017 after reaching the finals but she just couldn't cross the line. She will probably achieve more after she retires. Mithali has Saturn and Neptune exalted in her horoscope. That means Saturn will give her success later in life. Therefore, any option from coaching to administration would still be available to her and she could do a good job of it.

Mithali has a large karmic quota left and Indian cricket should benefit from that. She could still be around youngsters and groom them to become better cricketers. She would make a fantastic coach.

Mithali could also take up some important role in the BCCI and push the agenda for women's cricket. She will be around impacting the game for a very long time. While a biopic is being made on her, the makers may miss a few chapters she is yet to script.

Prediction #22

What Will Happen to Shikhar Dhawan?

Shikhar has played exceptionally well in the ICC tournaments and hence has managed to make a place for himself. He was the highest scorer for India in the 2015 World Cup, Down Under and was also the man of the series in the 2013 Champions Trophy that India won. Now, expecting him to do well once again in another ICC tournament would be asking for the moon. Besides, he also played a major part for the IPL-winning team, Sunrisers Hyderabad, in 2016. Shikhar's chart clearly shows that being the Man-of-the-Series in the 2013 Champions Trophy was the highest point of his career and he cannot better that.

It implies that Shikhar may not do very well in the 2019 World Cup. What we need to understand here is that if a player does not have the best planetary position at the time of a World Cup, it doesn't mean that they will fare badly in the tournament. In fact, that player may even go on to score a century or grab five wickets in the finale. But the very presence of that player distorts the astrological balance of the team and, collectively, the team may fail. Ironical, but that's how it works. Mahela Jayawardene scored a century in the final of the 2011 World Cup. But Dhoni's 91 was enough to win the match and the Cup.

In fact, if one of the players with a weaker horoscope starts performing well in the tournament, you can be sure that that team will find it difficult to win. For example, in the 2015 World Cup, the batsmen with the best horoscopes from the Indian contingent were Rohit Sharma and Virat Kohli. But Shikhar Dhawan was the one who grabbed the limelight with exceptional performances. When something like this happens, you know that the team will not do well.

Contrarily, the player with one of the best horoscopes for Australia, Steven Smith, performed well for them and then you knew that their chances were higher.

Also, the presence of all the players who have already achieved what their horoscope promised can only pull the team down.

So, in the 2019 World Cup, if Shikhar starts doing well, it should be a worrying factor for India. That may mean that India will not win the Cup. If he doesn't do well, it will anyway put pressure on the middle order, especially on MSD, who would then have to get into the rescue mode. And he may not always be able to pull the team out of the woods, most importantly, when it matters the most.

Coming back to Shikhar, his performances in World Cup 2019 may not be satisfactory and he may slowly be ignored in the ODIs with the emergence of younger batsmen. Slowly but steadily Dhawan would disappear from the scene in both the tests and the ODIs. He would have a relaxed and fantastic life in Australia though after his retirement.

Prediction #23

What Will Ashwin Do?

Ravichandran Ashwin has an awesome horoscope. The 1986-born has an exalted Uranus, an exalted Neptune, Planet-Z and Planet-X. He will certainly become one of the greatest cricketers to have played for India. Of late, Ashwin has been cold shouldered by the Indian team and he no longer plays in the shorter formats of the game. This may work as a blessing in disguise for the Chennai man. His karmic quota is focused on one area, that is tests, and that means he has chances of doing exceedingly well there.

In the final analysis, while he will surpass Harbhajan's tally of 417 Test wickets beyond doubt, he may fall short of Kumble's 619. But his feats will be a tad greater than all the other spinners, for he would take those wickets in fewer test matches over fewer playing years.

In fact, Ashwin may end up being the second best bowler in the history of Indian cricket. Make no mistake about it, he is going to be around for sometime as the planet Uranus will be in a very good position for him till 2024. He can create magic until that time.

Despite the disadvantage of starting late in test cricket—at the age of 25 compared to 18 of Harbhajan Singh and 20 of Anil Kumble and Muttiah Muralitharan—Ashwin has been the fastest to reach 50, 100, 150 and

200 wickets. His strong planets indicate that he will continue to do the same en route to his 300, 400 and 500 wickets as well. Despite the presence of two young spin players in the squad, Ashwin will still shine in the test arena. He will continue to take wickets all around the world even in the most difficult of situations.

Besides taking wickets he will also contribute profusely with his bat and will probably end up being one of the best all rounders ever. Expect a few more centuries from him.

The Chennai lad's captaincy skill is another area the world is yet to discover. Expect Kings XI Punjab to reap the benefits of his shrewd mind. Any IPL team that has Ashwin as their captain has a great chance to win the tournament. Remember, a 1986-born has to win the next two or three IPLs and Ashwin has great chances as he has a brilliant horoscope and he doesn't captain elsewhere. Also, just like Kumble this engineer may land a chance to lead India in tests for a brief while at some point of the team's transition or due to injury or rest to the regular captain, Kohli.

Ashwin should have a very good career post retirement. Expect him to have some radically different business ideas compared to most other retired cricketers and he would make a super-successful businessman. Above all, he will also be giving back to the game that has made him what he is in a big way either in the form of a coach or a facilitator. His Planet-Z would ensure that he is a great mentor and teacher. He would identify young talent and nurture it to success. His academy would become one of the best in the country and he has great chances of becoming the Pullela Gopichand of cricket.

Prediction #24

Will David Warner Win Another IPL?

David Warner has an extraordinary birth chart for sure. He has Uranus and Neptune as well as Planet-X in exaltation, and Mars and Venus in very powerful positions, making it a powerhouse of a chart. He also has the most powerful planet in the universe, Pluto, in deep debilitation that has made him go astray at times.

One can only feel sorry for him, because so many other sportsmen have gone scot-free even after committing crimes of much greater magnitude.

This incident left Warner and his family shattered and he has been through the worst phase of his life. How the mighty have fallen! The man who was destined to be one of the greatest players ever for Australia may not be their best ever. Worse still, one who had the potential to be their best captain ever, won't captain them ever again. That is a very sad thing for Warner.

I am not justifying Warner's actions here but, astrologically speaking, this could be the best thing that has happened to him. The biggest positive factor that arises from this is that Warner still has loads of karmic quota left. He may not be the Australian captain anymore, but he could still captain an IPL team. The

1986-born has a horoscope equivalent to Rohit Sharma's or even Virat Kohli's. So, the entire power of his planets will now be channelled through the IPL. A wounded Warner will be even more dangerous.

Even as a player he could be of extraordinary help if Kane Williamson captains SunRisers Hyderabad. Hyderabad has better chances if Warner is made the captain. Kane does have a fab horoscope and he could always be a future captain. But Warner needs to captain the team now to unleash his full potential. Simply by being the captain he would lead his team to stupendous victories. Warner is here to stay in the IPL and destined to win more as a captain; at least one more IPL title, either with SRH or any other team who will make him their captain.

Prediction #25

Is There Danger of Virat Becoming Another Tendulkar or a Messi?

I used to steal time to watch Tendulkar's innings in the 1990s. Later on I would follow the live online commentary of the matches. If it was a T20 match, with some relevance, I would also watch the second innings on TV. If it involved my predictions, then I might keep a tab on the matches, but did not necessarily take time to watch them. Nor did I watch any other sport. No tennis. No football.

As most football matches are late night affairs, I rarely catch them live even now. If there is one sportsperson I love to watch online these days, again and again, allowing YouTube to put the videos on loop, then it has to be Lionel Messi.

I am not sure what endears Messi to us—his 'messi-merising' passes and breathtaking goals or his humble background or his controlled aggression. And yes, there is this one anguish I share with most other Messi fans—I feel sorry that he couldn't win a major tournament for Argentina. I fantasised about him lifting the FIFA World Cup in 2014. Even in 2018, during the start of the World Cup, when my analysis clearly pointed to a 1986- or 1987-born as winning the Cup—and it finally boiled down to France and

Argentina—I secretly hoped, wished and prayed that it would be Argentina and not France. When France finally won the World Cup, it was more of a relief than happiness, as Messi hadn't gone down as the greatest ever. But isn't he the greatest?

Perhaps, he still could win a Copa America as a captain, but that wouldn't be equivalent to winning a World Cup and Maradona will still have the bragging rights as the greatest ever and that will be annoying.

Messi has great individual records but doesn't have a World Cup to boot. Even Tendulkar faced that for a long time. After coming back empty handed in five straight World Cups, Tendulkar was over the moon when he won the World Cup finally. Yes, now he has that most important thing he always wanted. To be known as a World Cup-winner. It came in his sixth attempt!

Seeing Virat Kohli scoring runs and breaking each and every record Sachin Tendulkar has ever made, I have a few worries. I secretly wish Virat wouldn't better Tendulkar, otherwise he would end up being another Messi.

I mean, we need to realise that one person cannot win everything in life. A sportsperson cannot be on the top in every aspect of a game, especially if there is another one around with a very similar horoscope.

To put things in perspective, there were three players who had equal chances of winning the 2018 football World Cup—Spain's Sergio Ramos (1986), Argentina's Lionel Messi (1987) and France's Hugo Lloris (1986). All three had the best horoscopes—the best in the world. But Lloris won it because he had nothing else to show for his achievement. Messi was already one of the greatest ever with record goal scoring; Ramos had already won three Champions League titles as captain hence, the trophy had to go to Lloris as the natural equaliser.

If Virat becomes the greatest ever in terms of run making or any other achievement that is tough for someone else to surpass, then his chances to win a world Cup as a captain will go down for two reasons. One, he has already won a World Cup as a player—the same that Tendulkar, too, won. Two, he is the greatest player ever. So, the World Cup-winning captain would be someone else as an equaliser by the universe. Remember, the greatest ever players we have had in our country have never won a World Cup as captains—Sunil Gavaskar and Sachin Tendulkar! I'm afraid Virat is in danger of going that way.

Strange, I know, but that is how it works. So, the question is, do we want to see Virat as the greatest ever cricketer or a World Cup-winning captain? Both, I'm sorry folks, may not happen. It has not happened with Messi and Tendulkar and may not with Virat either.

Prediction #26

Can Virat Better Tendulkar's Records?

As a chemistry student, I was in awe of isomers. I did not know I would encounter something similar when I studied astrology. For people with no background in science, an isomer is a molecule with the same molecular formula as another molecule, but with a different chemical structure. Isomers contain the same number of atoms of each element, but the atoms have different arrangements.

This is really uncanny. Virat Kohli's horoscope can be called an isomer of Sachin Tendulkar's. It is a mirror image. The strongest planets in Sachin's chart are the same as in Kohli's. Sachin has Planet-X (2007 RH283) in exaltation, Virat does too. Sachin has Uranus in exaltation, and so does Virat. Sachin has Mars in exaltation, ditto for Virat! While the Little Master has Planet-Z (2008 FC76) in its own house, the younger champion has Planet-Z in exaltation. Nothing to choose between the two, really. Yes, a planet's *exaltation* is always better as compared to it being in its *own* house—and therein lies the key difference between the two great players.

So, the end result will be the same. If Sachin has attained greatness already, Virat too, will. At the end of his career, Virat will retire as one of the greatest to have graced the game of cricket. Exactly as Tendulkar did. So, the end picture is clear; now we only need to fill in the details. We know the climax of the story; we need to know the various interesting episodes that will dot the storyline.

While the date of birth does give some idea about the extent of grandeur a sportsperson will enjoy, the biggest clue to their greatness comes from their date of debut. The debut is like a second birth for the sportsperson. The fascinating thing I have observed is that the greatest sportspersons make their debuts under the auspices of the most magical planetary configurations.

Let us look at the test debut dates of two of the greatest Indian cricketers before Virat arrived on the scene.

Sunil Gavaskar: 6th March 1971

Sachin Tendulkar: 15th November 1989

This may sound like a bit of mumbo jumbo to the uninitiated, but will shock people who do know some astrology. The astonishing bit about Sunil Gavaskar's birthday (10th July 1949) is that he was born when Pluto had just entered its exaltation zodiac sign, Leo, after about 260 years! This was an extraordinary phenomenon. The initial phase of the exaltation of Pluto is called the 'eagle' phase. People born in this period go on to achieve success, fame and power that seem to arise out of nowhere. Rajinikanth and Narendra Modi are some other examples of eagles in their respective domains.

Sunil Gavaskar created a record of 34 test centuries, which stood unbroken for more than two decades, until the Little Master arrived on the scene. Gavaskar was the first man to reach 10,000 runs in test cricket, which was simply the eagle effect of Pluto. That cannot be taken away from him.

Now, look at the debut date of Gavaskar—6th March 1971. Did you notice something? This is just a couple of years apart from Sachin Tendulkar's birthday—24th April 1973.

Now, when you examine the planets of Tendulkar's chart at his birth, what do you see? Uranus in exaltation, Planet-X in exaltation, Planet-Z in its own house. Exactly the same planet arrangement as on Sunil Gavaskar's debut date!

This implies that when Sunil debuted, the planets indicated that he would create a revolutionary record (34 centuries and 10,000 runs) due to the exaltation of Uranus, and would achieve superstardom due to the exaltation of Planet-X, and Planet-Z being in its own house, both the planets indicating monetary success and personal glory respectively.

The major planets remain almost in the same place for about two or three years. Simply put, *Gavaskar's debut = Tendulkar's birth.* So, astrologically, this means Tendulkar was destined to become Gavaskar's natural successor. He was the *chosen one*!

And what happened next?

Sachin Tendulkar debuted on 5th November 1989, when Pluto entered its own zodiac sign, Scorpio, after 260 years! What a celestial marvel. Both Gavaskar and Sachin share the magic of Pluto and Uranus. Pluto indicates the introduction of new paradigms and the end of the old order. Uranus brings in innovation, newness and the breaking of old customs.

Gavaskar performed the feat for the first time; Sachin broke that record and created a new score in its place, and rewrote history books. Both managed to pull off the same *tour de force* due to the same set of planets.

The magic didn't end there.

Three years before Sachin Tendulkar debuted—on 15th November 1989, a certain Virat Kohli was born in Delhi, on 5th November 1986, with almost the same set of planets that Sachin had at the hour of his debut! *Tendulkar's debut = Kohli's birth!*

Since Virat Kohli has almost the same horoscope as Sachin, it means he should be his natural successor, just as Sachin was Gavaskar's.

(Virat's track record in the national and international cricket arena, and the trajectory of his overall success, can be ascribed to the same planetary arrangement as that of Sachin at the time of his debut. After establishing a similar and astonishing planet nexus in case of Gavaskar and Sachin, it is hard to believe that the repeat is not true in case of Sachin and Virat. According to astrology, then, Virat should ideally be a 1986-born—the time which ties in neatly with how his life has played out so far—though the official records put his date of birth at 5th November 1988.)

A miracle, isn't it?

The groundbreaking Uranus will help Virat break all previous records, including the highest number of test as well as ODI centuries by Sachin, and also the highest test and ODI runs scored. All the four records are in danger of being surpassed by Virat and each will be a wonderful conquest if it happens.

Let us examine Virat's debut dates to see how much of this is possible.

Test debut of Virat Kohli: 20th June 2011

ODI debut of Virat Kohli: 18th August 2008

The test debut happened on a day when Planet-X and Planet-Z were in deep exaltation simultaneously in Pisces. This is phenomenal indeed. Pisces symbolises the deep sea and the achievements connected to Planet-X in Pisces and Planet-Z in Pisces are almost oceanic! The last time Planet-X was in Pisces in deep exaltation was way back in 1946, and that year produced three American presidents—Bill Clinton, George W Bush and (surprise!) Donald Trump. Not an ordinary planetary position at all. Easy to deduce that Virat Kohli can surpass Sachin's 51 test centuries and 13,000 runs in test cricket.

Besides, since Virat also had Venus and Mars in conjunction on that debut day, it only goes to show that he will achieve his milestones in test cricket after fighting hard battles. No wonder he loves to go for a win in test matches rather than settle for a draw.

Look at Virat's ODI debut that happened when Uranus was in its own house after 84 years and Planet-X was still in the oceanic Pisces! Now that is phenomenal too. I'm falling short of adjectives now. In ODI cricket, it is very simple. Kohli will not just break old records, but will create his own, which will be very tough to beat.

So, will Kohli break Tendulkar's records? Of course, he will. Definitely. *Pakka* promise! All the records of

Tendulkar from the hundred 100s, the highest scorer in tests, the highest test and ODI centuries, the highest run getter in ODIs, the highest number of 50s, well all of these and many more of Sachin's records are in danger. Virat will better many records of Sachin and faster. The legend of Virat Kohli will only grow—and stay for a long time to come.

Could someone beat Virat's records?

Of course. Virat debuted in 2008. Someone born two-three years earlier, that is in 2004–06, could go on to beat Virat's records. The show will go on.

Prediction #27

What Will Rohit Sharma Do?

Rohit Sharma is probably the best captain India never had. He could have been a deadly captain, emulated MSD and won at least one World Cup for India. Unfortunately, he could never become the regular captain of India in either format, with the imposing Virat Kohli still around.

India's loss was Mumbai Indians' gain and Rohit has already notched up three IPL victories for them. One important factor in the horoscope of the 'hitman' that offers hope is that despite being a part of World Cup victory, he didn't play a huge role in the 2007 T20 World Cup win and he wasn't even part of the 2011 World Cup win. It suggests that he could play a huge role in another World Cup, which India may win.

Now, this is stupendous. If there is some way Rohit could be made the captain of the Indian team, especially in one of the two T20 World Cups coming up in 2020 and 2021, then India stands a great chance to win it. Rohit has proved to be a calm captain with a strong mind while captaining Mumbai Indians and also during the Asia Cup that he led to victory in 2018. We need that. He has the required planets too, which is a bonus.

Alas, this is only a fantasy so far. Rohit is still being branded as a limited-overs specialist, but he can actually be an excellent test player. He has developed the habit of posting ridiculously good scores in limited-overs cricket, but he has been tentative in tests. He needs to be given an extended run in the tests since he has the capacity to change the rules of the game. In tests, Rohit can at least do half of what he has done in the ODIs. He can be the ideal number 6, coming in before Rishabh Pant. He can also be given the license to go for the kill as an opener in the tests. His overseas records are going to grow during the next three years. He may be just the batsman Kohli needs if they want to continue winning overseas. In the IPL, he can just go on and even win another title, but probably with a different coach.

India needs Rohit. They need to find a way to extract the maximum out of him as a captain in any format so that we can have another chance to win a title. He also needs to be in the test squad. Sacrifice an opener, an all rounder or whatever but give Rohit some confidence and back him up and he will play astounding test cricket for another five years.

Prediction #28

What is the Future of Pujara?

The Man-of-the-Tournament in the historic 2018–19 Test Series victory in Australia showed the immense value that he brings to the table. With his impeccable performance, Cheteshwar trashed all the talks of his slow batting and won back the confidence of the captain and the coach who had dropped him in the crucial test matches (and probably the series) in South Africa and England in 2018. With his exemplary performance, he showcased how test cricket should be played. He is splendid for these times of instant cricket. But, will he be the greatest of all time? Maybe not.

One interesting common factor between Cheteshwar and the greatest number 3 of all time for India, Rahul Dravid, is that both of them have their moon in the zodiac sign, Pisces. Pisces is a water sign. Water takes the shape of the container it is filled in. Similarly, Rahul Dravid and Cheteshwar Pujara can mould themselves according to the circumstances and keep batting, regardless of how difficult the situation is. Pisceans learn from their past mistakes and repeat them very rarely. Dravid and Pujara improvised and performed very well in the grounds and conditions that they didn't do as well in their first attempts.

The difference between Cheteshwar Pujara and Rahul Dravid is that the latter has a superior horoscope. Rahul also debuted on an extraordinary date, which ensured that he remained the mainstay of India's batting for a very long time, even in the ODIs. Pujara can finally say that he has established ownership over the number 3 position in the tests, but he has been ignored completely in the ODIs. Pujara will certainly not surpass the greatness of Rahul Dravid, even in the tests. However, his date of debut does show that he will constantly face difficult situations and do a great job under pressure. He will win many matches for India on his own like he did against Australia in 2018–19. The Saurashtra lad has a couple of such heroics in his chart. He will be around for a few more years and be a reliable batsman, one down, for quite some time.

Fortunately or unfortunately for Pujara, he plays only test cricket. This is a blessing in disguise for him as his karmic quota of success is only utilised there and will add to the total tally. Pujara will go down in history as one of the greatest one-down players ever for India. He can never ever displace Rahul Dravid either in the number game, that is runs scored, or in quality or the circumstances under which the runs were scored. But let's stop the comparison here and let Pujara be his own man. Pujara being himself is of immense value to Indian cricket. And he will go on battling it out for the team in the only way he knows—bringing the team to a position of strength.

Can Pujara play ODIs? Of course, he can. You need a player who can stabilise the innings in case there is a collapse. In these times of the T20, when the players have forgotten the art of playing long innings, Cheteshwar can be the key. Battling for 50 overs is a long time and Pujara can hold one end up, while the batsmen at the other end go berserk with their bat. The challenge here is that many players are knocking on the doors of ODI cricket and he may end up playing only tests. That may not be a bad thing. When he finally hangs up his boots around 2023–24, he may be the last of the vintage icons of test cricket.

Prediction #29

What Now for Bhuvneshwar Kumar?

Bhuvneshwar Kumar has been the answer to many scorching questions in Indian cricket for a while now. Unfortunately, a cruel turn of fate may steal some of his thunder in the end analysis of his career.

Planet-Z in Bhuvi's birth chart is a powerful exoplanet in exaltation and Mars, the planet of power, is in its own house. The Uttar Pradesh youngster has all his personal planets in Capricorn, making him industrious, disciplined and responsible. He has also been bestowed with maturity beyond his age and the temperament to excel at the highest level.

The only bowler to dismiss Tendulkar for a duck in domestic cricket has all the astrological markings required for a genuine all-rounder. He has impressed everybody with his swing and movements in bowling. Many a time he has also rescued his team from precarious situations with his sensible batting. The soft-spoken youngster has seen phenomenal growth since his debut in 2012, helping India win many matches.

One major problem in Bhuvi's horoscope though is that he was born on an *Amavasya* or new moon day. An *Amavasya*-born cricketer has frequent breaks in his career either due to injuries or off-the-field controversies.

L Balaji, Shaun Marsh, Herschelle Gibbs, Marlon Samuels and Andrew Symonds are some examples.

The medium pacer from UP has chances of his career ending in a similar fashion as Balaji's or Shaun Marsh's, with some stupendous performances interspersed with long injury-related recovery periods. In fact, looking at the current flurry of speedsters in the Indian set-up, Bhuvi may find it difficult to hold his spot on for a long time. He may also be a disappointment in the World Cup 2019. India may miss the Bhuvneshwar of yore who was easily the spearhead of the Indian team. His jaded form is going to hurt India's chances now.

After a lacklustre performance in the showpiece event, Bhuvi will not be able to hold on to his position in the Indian team for too long. He has had a decent run in Indian cricket and filled in a void for some time, but he may have to make way for other cricketers who will deliver better. *Amavasya* can create other troubles too, which he needs to be wary of. One can just hope he doesn't go down as a fallen man, as no one would have toiled as hard and excelled so well, within his own limitations, as Bhuvi has.

Prediction #30

What Will Harmanpreet End up Doing?

When Indian women cricketers met the English in the World Cup finals of 2017, it was an easy prediction for me. Harmanpreet Kaur had played a whirlwind innings in the semi-finals and taken India to the finals. But the final contest was simply between the two captains, Heather Knight and Mithali Raj. Mithali could never have vanquished Heather who had a superior horoscope.

Well, now Harmanpreet has become the skipper of the T20 team and her horoscope matters instead.

Harmanpreet has one of the best horoscopes amongst the Indian women cricket squad. In fact, the horoscope is so phenomenal that it could be called *the* best. Harmanpreet will do something exceptional—far better than whatever she has done before and she has done quite a lot. She was the first Indian woman to score a T20 century, the first to be signed on by an overseas T20 team; she has the highest individual score in a knockout match in the women's World Cup.

All these accomplishments could pale in comparison to what she could still achieve in cricket. She could reach the pinnacle in women's cricket in India. She could change the way Indian women's cricket is viewed and played. Just like what the 1983 World Cup win under Kapil Dev did for the men's team. She has exactly the same planet that propelled Kapil Dev to do what no Indian cricketer had done before. Harmanpreet, too, could do what no other Indian woman has done before.

How about winning the women's World Cup?

It doesn't matter which one it is—a 50-over or a T20. But Harmanpreet has it in her to be the first Indian woman cricketer to win the World Cup as a captain. Yes, she does. Harmanpreet will go down in history as one of the best female players India had ever produced by the sheer weight of her runs and wickets and especially the manner in which she scores them. A couple of women have been there before. We have had a few Goswamis, Eduljis, Kulkarnis, Raus, Jains, Chopras and Rajs. But Harmanpreet will go where none of these cricketers have gone before.

The *Arjuna Award* winner has Pluto entering its own house after 260 years, and Planet-X and Planet-Z in exaltation, which show that she will be the greatest ever. The extraordinary placement of Mars and Venus in conjunction in the eighth house indicates her conquering enemies. Neptune exalted in the seventh house indicates the possibilities of her being a world champion. Interestingly, her Planet-X is her twelfth lord and is deeply exalted. The twelfth house indicates glory in a foreign land. The next two women's World Cups, the T20 and the 50-over, are scheduled to happen in Australia and New Zealand in 2020 and 2021 respectively. Is there a historic moment waiting for India in either of these years? Possible, very possible!

Harmanpreet could make it happen. She could forge an extraordinary partnership with the 1965-born coach, WV Raman, and create magic.

Raman, despite his impressive horoscope, couldn't achieve much as a player. Yes, he was the coach of the Tamil Nadu, West Bengal and a few IPL teams and also did a stint at the National Cricket Academy (NCA) in Bangalore. But he hasn't done anything really spectacular as a coach either so far. The man who was born in the same year as the Khans in Bollywood and the Waughs in cricket has a big moment in his life which is yet to manifest itself. Don't forget, Raman too has Pluto's power in his favour.

Together with the best woman cricketer ever in Harmanpreet, he could script one of the greatest stories ever in Indian women's cricket! I'm waiting with bated breath. Just like I did in 2011.

sportskeeda

ICC Women's World Cup 2017: Scientific Astrologer predicts India to fall short at the final hurdle

Greenstone Lobo FOLLOW
ANALYST

Feature
15.92K // 22 Jul, 2017
< SHARE

Who will come out on top in the summit clash?

Prediction #31

How Far Can Yuzvendra Chahal Go?

A spinner needs to read the mind of the batsman/woman. A fast bowler can intimidate them with pace, bounce and swing, but the spinner essentially plays with the batsman's mind. Yuzvendra Chahal has that ability in abundance with his major planets in the zodiac sign, Cancer. He has remarkable sensitivity and understanding of the mind of many a batsman and surprises them with his wrist movements.

One thing that will stand out for Chahal is that he will be one spinner equally effective under home conditions that are spinner-friendly as well as international conditions—on pitches which may not help spinners naturally. He has a rare fourth house with Jupiter exalted there, making him successful in the country of his birth. He will also create some memorable success stories internationally because of the twelfth Lord (of international success), Neptune, being exalted in the ninth house (of foreign countries).

Chahal will undoubtably be one of the best bowlers to have played for India. He is definitely going to break many records. He is going to be a World Cup-winner as well.

Chahal needs to safeguard his financial interests because the only things that he can be successful in life are those connected with cricket. He will be a master of his art and a super achiever at it and will not need to do anything else in life. Unlike other players, who succeed in business or other ventures, Chahal may not have a huge success. His success after retirement can come from teaching his art to youngsters or as a commentator. So, he needs to maximise his playing years and invest carefully. In fact, the best of his career is yet to start and it will see steep success from 2021 to 2025. He will form a great partnership with the chinaman bowler, Kuldeep Yadav, and both of them will strangle the opposition in tandem and put India on top. Both Kuldeep and Yuzvendra will stay relevant till some players born after 2000 make their debut post 2021.

Prediction #32

Will Karun Nair Bounce Back?

I find it extremely painful when I see the brilliant horoscopes of umpteen youngsters who have superb talent but fall off the radar because someone else has a slightly better horoscope than them. All the talent in the world cannot take you to the next level if luck is not with you. Also, only 11 players can play for a team at any time. Cruel!

Karun Nair must easily be one of the best young talents in the country. He made an extraordinary start to his career by slamming a triple century in only his third test match for the country against England in 2016. However, the next few outings didn't yield too many runs for him. Except for the triple century his average was unremarkable. But, as a triple century-hitter, he certainly deserves more chances.

To the dismay of even stalwarts like Sunil Gavaskar and Dilip Vengsarkar, he was dropped from the test team that played against the West Indies. He was still in the squad but, ignoring him, the selectors gave Hanuma Vihari a test debut out of the blue. Vihari grabbed the opportunity with both hands and made a fighting half century, which saved the test match. Nair didn't find himself in the squad that went to Australia and conquered them on their own soil either. Mayank

Agarwal made his debut in the series and gave a good account of himself. That has only made things tougher for Karun.

So what is the road ahead for him? While there is no question that Karun Nair has great talent, the planets in his chart are working against him. Unfortunately for Karun, he was born on *Amavasya,* hence a weak sun and moon. He also has Planet-X and even Uranus in debilitation. Four important planets in such weak positions are pulling him down.

The ill placement of the planets shows that even if Nair is given another opportunity, his scores may not be compelling enough and he may soon be dropped once again, or he may fall out of favour with the selectors. Besides the weak planets, Karun also has to fight against a number of players who have better horoscopes than him. Who will he replace anyway? KL Rahul and Shreyas Iyer are just two examples that are snapping at his heels besides Hanuma Vihari. Also, he cannot replace Ajinkya Rahane, who is a proven performer. With Rohit Sharma set to receive more opportunities to establish his credentials as a test player, Nair's chances appear even bleaker.

Not everything is lost for him though. He can still keep playing domestic cricket very well. He could be a domestic cricket icon easily enough—like Wasim Jaffer, Amol Mazumdar and a few others. He could also play county cricket and other domestic tournaments within other countries.

Karun will be an extremely important talent in domestic tournaments like the IPL. He will be one of the most important contributors to his team. He could even win an IPL as a player. Karun Nair may not be destined to be a cricket legend, but he will certainly make a mark. He could also be a good businessman, with special emphasis on import-export. Karun will also find success in the allied fields like entertainment and politics. Karun could also do a lot for the improvement of the game and be an outstanding commentator.

Prediction #33

Will KL Rahul Be Back?

It was always waiting to happen. KL Rahul was supposed to get into a huge mess, something which would almost derail his career. Planet-X is in a debilitated state in his third house. This house indicates communication (the tongue). Ironically, this house also indicates the hands. A naturally talented and gifted batsman, the captain and the team persisted with him, expecting him to deliver at some point. But Rahul had a forgettable 2018, except a fantastic IPL outing. He has been going through one of the worst phases of his career (a carry-over in 2019) and couldn't justify his talent or the faith of the team. And the worst was yet to come; he found himself embroiled in a controversy together with his teammate, Hardik Pandya, about their callous and misogynistic comments on a television chat show.

At the moment I write this, Planet-X is transiting its own house and is in a position exactly opposite to what it was at Rahul's birth. Rahul found himself in trouble regarding both his hands and his tongue. He didn't do well with the bat and said something which went against him or, rather, he didn't speak up when he should have. People who have seen the video would have noticed that it was Hardik Pandya who made all the damaging statements. Unfortunately, Rahul's silence made him an accomplice, because he didn't object to the things Pandya said.

No one would disagree with the fact that, as a cricketer, Rahul has class. He has substance enough to make a comeback. In fact, he will. Not only will he do it, but he will do it in style. He has enough grit to become one of the most iconic players in Indian cricket history. In the next few years he will put his head down and come back to prove his mettle.

Rahul's horoscope has Neptune in the deepest exaltation, Pluto in its own house, Planet-Z in exaltation, an exalted Venus and even the sun. So it is unquestionably an extremely powerful chart. Rahul has such an amazing horoscope that its really difficult to predict how far he can go in this career. Looking at the fact that he is still so young, there are several possibilities. First of all, he will score well when he makes his comeback. The years after 2020 will see Rahul on a roll. He will slowly but steadily cement his place once again in all the formats of the game. He could also become the captain of an IPL team. The chances are quite bright. In fact, if Virat Kohli decides to quit his captaincy, Rahul will become his natural successor. Yes, at this point of time it may seem too far-fetched, but Rahul could indeed become the captain of the Indian cricket team in one of the formats. If he doesn't become the captain, then one thing is for sure. He will go on to be one of the most scintillating Indian cricketers ever. So Rahul will not just be back, but he will stay for a long time—and successfully.

Prediction #34

Will Bumrah Be a Cricket Legend?

So will Jasprit Bumrah will be a cricket great? Yes, definitely!

For people interested in statistics I have something interesting. The greatest fast bowler of India, Kapil Dev, debuted for India in October 1978—in the same month the second-best fast bowler in the country, Zaheer Khan, was born. Uncanny, isn't it?

Now Zaheer Khan debuted for India in late 2000. Probably, somewhere around that time, one of the greatest fast bowlers for India should have been born.

So, going by reverse logic, did any great fast bowler debut for India during the time when Jasprit Bumrah was born—in December 1993? Well, no one in India. However, this is a great patch astrologically—late 1993. Pluto was in its own house, Planet-X was in exaltation and planet Neptune was in the deepest exaltation. Some great guy must have debuted somewhere.

Yes, one man did. Glenn McGrath! One of the greatest fast bowlers in the world debuted exactly in the same week as Jasprit Bumrah's birth. I should say it the other way around. Bumrah was born exactly in the week when the great McGrath debuted for Australia. Well, that is something.

That implies Jasprit will go on to acquire great stature for sure. His horoscope indicates the possibility of him overtaking even Zaheer Khan in the list of the all-time greats for India. He may fall behind Kapil Dev, who will remain India's greatest fast bowler ever. There are massive possibilities for Bumrah. While Pluto and Neptune in his chart are similar to Kapil Dev's, he has Venus and Mars in conjunction, like Zaheer. So, while he may produce some extraordinary spell bamboozling batsmen to throw their wickets away, he can also toil hard and earn his wickets under extremely tough conditions and circumstances. This also implies he will do well in the Indian sub-continental pitches too which assist spin more than pace.

The year 2019 started on a good note for Bumrah and he will do well for a decade or more. In the years after 2021, he will become even more dangerous. He is already one of the best bowlers in the world and will terrorise batsmen around the world from 2021 to 2027. Injuries might slow him down somewhat. But being the wily bowler that he is, he will compensate for that with his clever bowling, outsmarting the batsmen.

Bumrah's final wickets tally will be lower than Kapil Dev's but higher than Zaheer Khan's. There is no question that Jasprit Bumrah will end up being one of the best bowlers of his generation and an inspiration to many budding fast bowlers from India. And yes, if Virat has to win a World Cup, he cannot do it without Bumrah in the playing XI.

Prediction #35

Shreyas Iyer—How Big Will He Be?

Shreyas Iyer is going to be huge. Really huge. He has a fantabulous horoscope. He is the future of Indian cricket. We all know he has great talent. The important question is: does he also have the luck to shine as a star?

He has six planets in positions of strength—Pluto, Neptune, Planet-X, Planet-Y, Chiron and Venus. That is something. He is bound to be one of the biggest batsmen ever from India. He has not lived up to the promise of his chart so far, but his best is yet to come. The year 2020 will be the beginning of a splendid stretch for Shreyas Iyer. In the next decade, from 2021 to 2031, Shreyas will break many records and also create many of his own.

Shreyas has Pluto in the ascendant. It is the natural ruler of sports and it is in its own house after 260 years. This huge planet placed in the ascendant makes him potentially a great leader in sports. This indicates that he will not just be a batsman, but he could also assume bigger roles in cricket. Shreyas is obviously one of the future captains of India. He has already captained the Delhi Daredevils and if they persist with him, he could create absolute magic. Shreyas could be an extraordinarily successful captain.

It is very difficult to find a player who can do justice to his role as a team player as well as the captain, simultaneously. A few well-known names are Virat Kohli, MS Dhoni and Sourav Ganguly. Yes, it is too early to say this but that is the rare combination Shreyas Iyer possesses. The exalted Planet-Y and Chiron in eleventh house also indicate that he will play for a very long time. He is quite young now. That means he could keep going until his late thirties.

Shreyas Iyer's successes will prompt big brands to hire him as an ambassador in the future. So, all you brand managers, catch him when he is still young, so that you can save some money!

Prediction #36

Will Hardik Pandya Beat Kapil Dev?

It is very unfair to compare Hardik Pandya with Kapil Dev. The young man doesn't want that to be done. He wants to be himself and be known for being himself—which is fair. Even Gavaskar has said, 'Kapil Dev is a one-in-a-century player and should never be compared; we should leave Hardik Pandya alone.'

Then why this comparison? It is to gauge, astrologically, how far Hardik Pandya can go.

Hardik's brilliant horoscope has Pluto in its own house, Neptune in exaltation and Planet-X in exaltation. These three planets are enough to make him a good all-rounder. But can these planets make him a great all-rounder in the mould of a Kapil Dev or a Richard Hadlee or an Ian Botham? No, not possible. All these great all-rounders had more planets in stronger positions. As an all-rounder one is expected to do well every time they are on the field. So the number of planets they require in high strength is much more. Hardik is found wanting in this respect. Hence, he will be a good all-rounder, but perhaps not a great one. He could be another Irfan Pathan or better, but not a Kapil Dev.

Also, Kapil Dev had a huge impact on the outcome of a game. Hardik Pandya may not have such kind of a huge impact. One very important planet for a fast bowler is Mars. It is the planet of stamina, energy and strength. Unfortunately, Mars is in a weak position in Hardik Pandya's chart. The weak Mars will ensure that he has frequent breakdowns and injuries that will impact his game. He will pick up some wickets in one match and score a few runs in the other, but consistency will be a challenge. In the long run, Hardik will be Hardik as he wants to be known. And, yes, he will come out of this school-boyish kind of attitude that got him into trouble and be sober and gentler.

Prediction #37

Who Will Be the Captain of India after Virat Kohli?

Now, this is the other question many have asked me time and again. While Dhoni was at the helm, it was very difficult to imagine another player who would go on to become the captain, replacing the Chennai Super King. That is, until Virat Kohli, with his cocksure attitude, slowly made the mantle of captaincy his own. Now, it is very difficult to think of someone as Virat's replacement, simply because it seems that Virat will remain the captain for another five years. Or at least until the 2023 World Cup, scheduled to be held in India.

Who indeed will wear the crown after King Kohli—say after 2023?

Well, as we have touched upon this earlier, it is KL Rahul. Shreyas Iyer, too, looks good enough to don the mantle. If the captaincy is split between these two gentlemen, it will be great for Indian cricket indeed.

After MS Dhoni and Virat Kohli, there seems to be no player over the horizon who has natural leadership abilities like these two greats of the game. Yes, there are some players who could be very good leaders, but they are still very young. Before a long-term captain can be appointed, there may be a phase where a couple of interim captains hold fort. Shreyas Iyer and KL Rahul could serve that purpose.

Rahul does have the captaincy element in him due to his extraordinary horoscope. He scores over all the other contenders simply because he wouldn't want to be one in the first place.

Mercury in Pisces also gives them the ability to absorb and learn from others, all the while being an excellent team player. You also need to give it to him that he has amazing maturity as a cricketer. He can be calm during a crisis. The sun in Aries gives him the leadership skills. So, if entrusted with the responsibility, Rahul can come up trumps. The Libra in him will ensure he is fair when he handles his team members.

On the other hand, Shreyas is a passionate Scorpio with the shrewd leadership skills of a Capricorn. He is the one you want when you go to war. Hence, both the boys are good contenders for the captaincy role. Let the best man win the crown. In fact, if both men win it, it will be a win-win situation for Indian cricket.

Prediction #38

How Far Will Kuldeep Yadav Go?

Kuldeep Yadav has a phenomenal horoscope. He has Pluto in its own house (of career). Pluto is the natural ruler of sports and having Pluto itself in your tenth house is an amazing piece of luck. Add to this the fact that Kuldeep also has Chiron in exaltation and Planet-Y in its own house—both in his eighth house (of sports) and we have a killer combination.

This extraordinary arrangement of planets is what makes him unique. He is the only chinaman bowler India has produced in ages. Kuldeep could probably be the best chinaman bowler ever in the world. In the process he could also go on to break many records and create a few of his own. He should also have a long career because of a very powerful eleventh house.

With Kuldeep there will be an additional bonus. Many may not have realised it, but he could also be a very handy batsman. He is an Aries-Scorpio. He has that fire in the belly. He was supposed to be a fast bowler but, at his coach's insistence, turned out to be a spinner. But his mind still works like a fast bowler's. He will come back at you if you you hit him hard. He can also whack the ball hard. He can be that healthy lower order batsman who adds some quick runs to your total.

While Kuldeep will do very well in tests, his greatness will be established in the limited-overs editions. He will certainly be a World Cup winner in one of these formats. He debuted on a full-moon day in the T20s and will go on to be a legend in that shortest format of the game.

Kuldeep will also be a very good businessman. His horoscope shows his excellent potential as a shrewd investor. He is going to be a wealthy man for sure.

Prediction #39

Is Smriti Mandhana Made for Bigger Things?

Smriti is meant for bigger things in life. Her remarkable horoscope has Planet-X in a rare exaltation in Capricorn. Besides that she also has Pluto, Planet-Y and Jupiter in their own houses. She is already doing pretty well for herself. The BCCI named her as the best woman cricketer in 2018. The ICC gave her the *Rachael Heyhoe-Flint Award* for the best cricketer of the year. Simultaneously, she was named the ODI player of the year.

Smriti's first breakthrough came in October 2013 when she became the first Indian woman to hit a double hundred in a one-day game. In 2016, Smriti also signed up with Brisbane Heat for the women's Big Bash League along with Harmanpreet Kaur—the first two Indians of either gender to sign up with them.

Smriti is going to be a pillar of strength for her skipper, Harmanpreet, and for India. If India is to win any big tournaments, it needs Smriti to play a crucial role. She missed the chance to create history when she got out for a duck in the 2017 cricket World Cup final against England. She had done well until then and her only failure robbed India of a great chance.

Smriti will not make the same mistake again. Together with Harmanpreet, she will be one of the highest run scorers for India. In all likelihood, she will also be one of the greatest openers from India. If India is ever to dream of winning a World Cup, then Smriti's should be the second name to feature on the list after Harmanpreet's.

Prediction #40

Who Will Be the Future Superstar of Indian Cricket?

Rishabh Pant for sure. Rishabh has an extraordinary horoscope with Pluto in its own house. Planet-Y, too, is in its own house. The most important aspect about his chart is that his birth coincides with the moment when Planet-X entered into deep exaltation. The nascent deep exaltation is very powerful and produces some titans. Rishabh will go on to be a superstar for certain.

He also has Venus and Mars in conjunction. Now this is a very important combination for a cricketer who would fight for victory against all odds. He may face impossible situations where he would have to either finish the game from an extremely difficult position or bide his time and slowly take his team to safety. Everyone loves a hero, isn't it? Especially one who can brave the odds and come out victorious. Rishabh will be that hero. This fire-fighter role will endear him to the masses and to the brands and he will undoubtedly be a huge brand magnet.

Rishabh's stocks will soar once be becomes an opener. Making him an opener will prove to be a fantastic decision by the Indian think-tank and will unlock his full potential. Rishabh can just destroy and demoralise the opposition with his murderous big hitting. He will remind us of some of the veteran Indian openers of yore and the entertainment and spunk associated with them. He will carve out a niche of his own though.

The fact that he will play all the three formats of the game would also work in his favour. So, be ready to see this young lad's face plastered on the billboards all over your city. His love life will be scrutinised and so will his every move. He will be an unexpected yet incredible fashion icon too. Yes, in 2021 and beyond, you will have a new cricket superstar in Rishabh Pant.

Prediction #41

Will These Two Late 1997-Borns Shine?

As I had mentioned many times before, the late 1997 patch would produce some sports greats in general and cricketing greats in particular. While Rishabh Pant is already there, we will also look at the possibility of two more promising talents in Khaleel Ahmed and Mayank Markhande.

Can Khaleel Ahmed be a great?

'Great' is a word we use very loosely. There are very few greats in fast bowling. One can call Courtney Walsh, Dennis Lillee, Richard Hadlee, Michael Holding, Andy Roberts, Malcolm Marshall and Wasim Akram as greats of fast bowling. But then so many others, who were very effective, cannot be called as greats. They did pick up wickets under tough situations, terrorised the best of batsmen and road-rolled over the opposition single-handedly many times. Some of them are Javagal Srinath, Venkatesh Prasad, Zaheer Khan, James Anderson, Dale Steyn, Glenn McGrath, Waqar Younis, Brett Lee and Shane Bond.

When one examines the horoscopes of most of the greats of the game, be it a batsman or a bowler, one finds that they had more than five planets in extremely strong positions at the time of their birth. Or they had great-impact planets like Pluto, Uranus or Neptune in the deepest exaltation. Sachin Tendulkar, Kapil Dev and MS Dhoni fall under this category.

Khaleel has three planets in strong positions. His Planet-X has just entered its nascent deep exaltation, planet Pluto is in its own house—and so is Planet-Y. This arrangement can make somebody a good, popular and an effective player but maybe not a 'great'.

Khaleel is a combination of Scorpio, Sagittarius and Capricorn. Scorpio and Sagittarius make him extremely passionate, full of energy and cool in temperament, but he is also blessed with a sharp mind because of Capricorn, which can help read the opposition very well. As he grows older and more mature, he will become a smart cricketer who will get wickets by deceiving the batsman then by felling them with his pace.

Khaleel may turn out to be one of the best, maybe one of the top 10 fast bowlers ever from India. He may not be a legend, but will be super effective. What's more, he could actually have something every great player would give their right arm to boast of—a place in a World Cup-winning squad!

What about Mayank Markhande?

My goodness, what a horoscope he has! India has an amazing pool of spinners that never dries. In Mayank Markhande, the latest addition, India seems to have fished out another winner. The young man was born in the last quarter of 1997, a deadly patch where some of the world's greatest sport stars must have been born. With the power of Pluto, Planet-X and Planet-Y, he also has Venus and Mars in conjunction. This connection is tremendous for fast bowlers. When a spinner has this combination, he can wreak havoc upon the opponents. Mayank should have the ruthlessness associated with fast bowlers. Add to it the fact that he is also a Scorpio-Pisces, two zodiac signs which are the epitome of guile, cunning and mystery—and he can simply hoodwink batsmen with these traits of a master spinner.

Mayank made a sensational debut for Mumbai Indians in 2018 and he will only get better each year in the club championship. He may become a veteran of the T20s. Expect him to become a permanent fixture in the T20 squad for India too, leading up to the next two World Cups in 2020 and 2021. India will have a strong spin triumvirate in Chahal, Yadav and Mayank. He will also feature in the ODIs soon. He is here for the long haul.

So, while Khaleel may not be termed as a great, he will still be an exciting talent for India who will do extremely well. Mayank, on the other hand, can really be up there as one of the best spinners to have played for India.

Khaleel and Mayank's horoscopes also suggest the possibility that a future Indian World Cup-winning squad is slowly being formed.

By the look of it, it seems India can have a World Cup-winning squad assembled just by having cricketers born in the years 1997–99.

Prediction #42

Will Prithvi Shaw Be Bigger Than Sehwag?

Interesting! People compare the young Prithvi Shaw with the veteran, Virender Sehwag. Gautam Gambhir has cautioned them against making such comparisons. He reasons that Prithvi had an easier outing against West Indies and he has tougher challenges ahead. He has a point there. Ganguly, too, has said that it is not fair to compare Prithvi with the genius, 100-test old Virender Sehwag.

I thought so too, but something very interesting caught my eye. Prithvi Shaw was born the year Virender Sehwag made his debut. It isn't really surprising that even Ravi Shastri has compared Prithvi with the veteran. As I have mentioned a few times in this book, if a future player is born at the time a great player makes his debut, it gives a fair indication of how far he would go.

When you dig deeper and focus minutely on Sehwag's debut day, you notice that it was 1st April 1999—an auspicious full-moon day! Yes, though Sehwag's debut coincided with Prithvi's birth in terms of the year, the planets over the horizon when the Nawab of Najafgarh debuted were super-extraordinary vis-à-vis those in Prithvi Shaw's birth chart. The X-factor of the full moon indicated Sehwag's longevity in the game and the amazing heights he reached. This extra zing that is missing in Prithvi's horoscope might have helped him perch next to the great icon. Also, when we go back to the basic birth charts, Prithvi Shaw has three planets in strong positions, while Sehwag had seven, so no comparison there either.

Ganguly and Gambhir are right. Prithvi will never be able to match the high levels the Sultan of Multan reached—not in his entire career. Besides, Sehwag had Venus and Mars in conjunction, the hallmark of a sportsperson who thrives, fights and wins against the toughest opposition. Prithvi will fall short slightly here too. But the fearless young man will carve his own niche. Let him be what he is supposed to be.

Prediction #43

Which Girls Will Make Indian Women's Cricket Soar?

The women's cricket team in India is oozing with talent. GenNext in the team seems very exciting with some superb players with incredible horoscopes. The younger players, if given enough chances, can easily replace the existing players successfully. They also have higher chances of winning a bigger tournament than their older sisters.

While Jemimah Rodrigues is a super-exciting talent amongst batswomen, the coach, WV Raman, would have a headache selecting a wicket keeper from amongst Ravi Kalpana, Nuzhat Parween and Taniya Bhatia. He could pick one of them as the wicket keeper and play the other two as specialist batswomen. All of them are very good and have equally marvellous horoscopes. The young bowlers, Radha Yadav and Pooja Vastrakar, also have unbelievable horoscopes which show that they will be around serving the country for a long time and successfully too.

One common factor noticeable in the horoscopes of all of these girls is that they are destined to bring a huge change in women's cricket. They also seem destined to achieve something bigger and take Indian cricket to the next level. These six girls would form the core of the team that catapults Indian women's cricket into a greater orbit. They will undoubtedly be finer achievers with greater glories in their kitty than their predecessors. With Harmanpreet at the helm, these six girls would bring in the much needed renaissance in the women's cricket in India. Watch out!

Prediction #44

Which Brothers Will Play for India and Do Well?

If we speak of international players who are brothers, Steve Waugh and Mark Waugh are at the top of the pyramid. Some other similar duos also played cricket at the same time, but not all of them were successful. In some cases one of the brothers did well and the other didn't. Irfan and Yusuf Pathan, Hardik and Krunal Pandya, Michael and David Hussey, Morné and Albie Morkel, Kamran and Umar Akmal are a few examples. One could also add Greg and Ian Chappel, Grant and Andy Flower to them. There is another pair from India that will be added to this list. Mark my words, both will play for India and do well too!

I am surprised this boy vanished from the scene after looking so promising. At the age of 12 he broke the record for the highest score in the Harris Shield Inter-school tournament in Mumbai, when he made 439 runs for Rizvi Springfield. He was always under the spotlight after that. Then he was acquired by Royal Challengers Bangalore and played well for them in his first season. Even Virat Kohli had admiration for him. The boy started off with a bang, but seems to be nowhere in the picture right now. There were doubts about the correctness of his year of birth and he had to undergo advanced tests to prove his age. I have his exact birth details and I can tell you that there is no iota of doubt regarding their authenticity as they clearly show the horoscope of a sportsperson.

He had to move away from Mumbai to Kashmir since his father and coach Naushad Khan felt he was not getting his due there. He was dropped by his IPL team, probably over issues regarding discipline and weight. He has been picked up by Kings XI Punjab in 2019 and, hopefully, he will remind people of his existence with a good show.

He hit those record runs during his schooldays and was marked as one for the future. But, as of now, he isn't anywhere on the scene. Mark my words now, he is definitely going to come back and will even go on to play for the country. He is Sarfaraz Khan.

When the parents of prospective cricketers come to me with the worry that their wards are doing well, but not well enough to be selected for domestic or IPL teams—or that the dream of playing for the country seems far away—I just have one thing to say to them. Remember that the timing of your child's success is already determined. You cannot force things to happen before their time. If your child has a good horoscope, but is not on the path to glory already, then you should know that his time has not yet come.

Pluto comes over the horizon in 2021 and Neptune in 2022. Believe me, some of the biggest cricketing stars will make their debut 2021 onwards—or, rather, 2022 and beyond.

If Sarfaraz Khan has not made his debut so far, it is good for him. A player who makes his debut in 2021 or 2022 or later will definitely be much more successful than someone who debuts for India now.

Talking about Sarfaraz, he has Pluto in its own house—his fifth house of fame in sports. Most importantly, Planet-X has entered its deepest exaltation in a nascent state. This powerful position can make someone a huge star. Note that Sarfaraz also has Venus and Mars in conjunction and he will go on to be the kind of player who rescues his team from the most difficult circumstances. Sarfaraz's chart also shows that he could be a part of a World Cup-winning team.

It seems Musheer, Sarfaraz's brother, has an even better horoscope with planet Pluto in its own house and Planet-X in the deepest exaltation! I really thank their father, Naushad Khan, for sharing their birth details, though reluctantly, after a lot of coaxing from me. Senior Khan has given birth to two gems! Both of them will go on to play for the country. Musheer is a talented spinner and all-rounder. It is very unfortunate that Musheer, a 12-year-old was banned by the MCA for three years for making obscene gestures at his opponent during a fight. A somewhat harsh verdict, I feel. I'm not sure about what Musheer will do and how the next three years will unfold for him, or even if the punishment meted out to him will be reconsidered. But one thing is for sure: his career will not be destroyed.

These brothers may not be on the cricket selectors' radar now. But, watch out, these two brothers *will* play for the country. They can even go on to be big stars. And, when they do, you will remember who told you about them first, won't you?

Prediction #45

Will India Ever Have Express Fast Bowlers Like Akhtar or Lee?

Will India ever have a fast bowler like Wasim Akram, Brett Lee or Shoaib Akhtar? Over the years many cricket fans have asked me this question and I'm going to answer it now. From the beginning Pakistan has been churning out fast bowlers and we have been doing the same with batsmen. Is there a possibility that we will produce at least one world-class, exceptionally fast bowler in the near future?

Funnily enough, the so-called fast bowlers we have had were actually medium pacers. Venkatesh Prasad, Javagal Srinath or even Zaheer Khan cannot categorically be classified as fast bowlers. In fact even the legendry fast bowler, Kapil Dev, lost pace after a few years. It was his sly swing bowling that gave him wickets and kept him going. Some people would say that Anil Kumble was the fastest bowler for India. Okay, just kidding. Yeah, we did have some real fast bowlers like Varun Aaron who could bowl over 150+ km per hour consistently, but they were very rare. As any good fast bowler would tell you, it is not simply pace that can fell a batsman. These pacers would have simply faded away if they hadn't been able to take wickets or had they been unidimensional.

We do have a good battery of fast bowlers right now. Jasprit Bumrah has been a revelation, Mohd Shami has been performing well—and young men like Khaleel Ahmed are also doing justice to their selection. So, finally, the pace department is looking good. I mentioned earlier that a great fast bowler was born in India during 2001–02, exactly around the time Zaheer Khan made his debut. This young boy will be a firebrand fast bowler and a great asset for India. There is also a chance that he could be born between 2003 and 2005 because this was the time when the planet, Pluto, was in its own house and Planet-X was in the deepest exaltation. While we have already identified one future great batsman of this generation of 2003–05 (explained in a later chapter) there is also a fast bowler—a real fast bowler—born in this generation. This boy would be about 13 years old now. I would urge the talent scouts to go and find this boy. He may be residing somewhere in a small town in India. They just need to find him.

Prediction #46

Will this Boy Make His Legendary Father Proud?

I'm not sure if life would be easy if you were the son of Amitabh Bachchan, Sunil Gavaskar, Rajiv Gandhi or Sachin Tendulkar. Maybe it would be slightly easier if you were the son of Kumaramangalam Birla. His son, Aryaman Birla, is trying his hand in a different field than his father—cricket. But the intense scrutiny you go through when your father is a legend in a particular field and the expectations to live up to the lofty standards set by your illustrious father can be really nerve-wracking. It is as if you have inherited them and you just have to go out there and start performing. Immense pressure—therefore—not easy.

Arjun Tendulkar has been making news simply because of his famous surname. Now, that may be a difficult cross to carry. But, Arjun Tendulkar will surely come out of the shadow of his legendary father and make a name for himself. The good thing is that there won't be an immediate comparison since he is not a batsman like his father, but rather a left-arm fast bowler who can also bat. He has successfully nullified any comparisons to start with. The only questions that remain to be answered now are whether he will play for India and, if so, will he do well? The answer to both is yes.

Arjun has Planet-X deeply exalted in his fourth house (of family), revealing his pedigree. It shows the immense strength in the areas of family wealth, upbringing, luxuries and vehicles. It simply means that he need not worry about making a living, but only needs to excel in his trade. Will he? That can be seen in his very first house that indicates 'personality'. It indicates who you are as a person and your individual strengths. The junior Tendulkar has the most powerful planet in the universe, Pluto, in its own house—the first house. Pluto is the natural eighth house ruler of sports and, when you have that planet in the first house in a strong position, then you are a gifted sportsperson.

This indicates that the junior Tendulkar will be good enough to play for India. Yes, without Papa Tendulkar having to coax anyone to allow his son to play. Arjun will take care of that slot all by himself. Left-arm seamers are a rare breed and he will make the best use of that void in India. He will perform fairly well in the international circuit. Expect him to play well in domestic tournaments like the IPL too. Some high points in his career will be really fantastic.

Will Arjun be a cricket great? No, not really. He won't be a Zaheer Khan or a Wasim Akram. Performance-wise he may be Ashish Nehra or Irfan Pathan's equivalent. He will never be able to match his father's stellar career—or smash records and create new ones like him. He won't be a legend, but he will surely be much more successful than most sons of famous fathers who have played cricket for India.

He will do what he has set out to do though—making his father proud.

Talking about sons making fathers proud, watch out for Aryaman Birla too! This gifted boy will make his businessman father proud with his exploits on the cricketing field.

Prediction #47

Will this Boy's Achievements Surpass His Father's?

Well, well, you need numerous planets to beat your father at his game, especially when he is a legend. And, if you plan to ply your trade following your father's footsteps, wouldn't he want his offspring to surpass him?

Many legendary fathers have tried every trick in the book to get their children to emulate them. Obviously, it is more common in the world of entertainment. But, if you wish to be as good as your father, then you need as good a set of planets as him. If you have better planets than your daddy, then, of course, you can outshine him in his field.

In the domain of entertainment, even if you inherit the looks of your good-looking father, you could still make it to an extent. But, in sports, it is all about skills. You need them in loads—and also the one ingredient that can change every equation—luck! You need that, too, in heaps to get things going your way.

Samit seems to have everything going for him. He is a Virgo-Libra-Sagittarius, which makes him a person inclined towards sports, naturally. Virgos are perfectionists, Librans have the artistry and style and Sagittarians are passionate. So, he is a born sportsman.

And he was born in the right home. His father is a legendary cricketer, revered for his professionalism, selflessness, the hard battles he fought on the field and the impeccable way in which he always conducted himself on or off it. Besides that, his father is also the coach of the junior Indian cricket team. He is going to learn the ropes from the best man in the country!

Samit has the requisite planets too, which means he has the luck. Look at that horoscope—he has Pluto coming into its own house, Planet-X in the deepest exaltation, Planet-Z in exaltation, Uranus in its own house, Planet-Y in its own house and Mars in its own house. That's phenomenal! And, you know what? Planet-X comes into the deepest exaltation once in about 63 years. Planet-X came into its deepest exaltation in 1942, when the Indian film legend, Amitabh Bachchan, was born.

Does Samit's birthday give something away? He was born on 11th October 2005, exactly 63 years after Mr Bachchan. This simply cannot be a coincidence. I hope Samit doesn't read this book, at least not yet. We don't want to put any pressure on that young boy. But I can just tell you that he has the capacity to become the Amitabh Bachchan of Indian cricket. Yes, that big! He is going to be a cricket-mammoth!

Samit will break records and tear his way into the history books. He will create his own records, too, which will stand for a long time. Mathew Hayden once said[1],

---

[1] Narayan, S. (2018, June 04). *5 life lessons given by Rahul Dravid*. Retrieved from: https://sportskeeda.com. Accessed on 17 February 2019.

'If you want to see aggression on the cricket field, look into the eyes of Rahul Dravid. He has the inner aggression. He doesn't show it by staring and chatting.' Samit will be a reflection of his father in this regard. He will be aggressive on the field, but still know where to draw the line. But he will be more flamboyant and forceful in his batting style than his technically correct father.

When Samit posts those big scores, makes a place for himself in the regional teams and then breaks into the national team, I hope people understand that it is through merit alone and not because of his father's clout. Samit has it all. His being born in Rahul Dravid's home at the right time was Destiny's sweet way of ensuring the continuity of his illustrious father's legacy.

Prediction #48

How Good Will the GenNext Be?

As we know, superstars in every field come in clusters. We have already discussed some of the major patches of greatness over the past century or so. Some great people were born in one generation, only to be surpassed by those born in another. We had the great Sunil Gavaskar and Kapil Dev ruling the 1970s and the 80s. Then, of course, came the wonderful generation of the 90s when we had the fab four: Sachin Tendulkar, Sourav Ganguly, VVS Laxman and, of course, Rahul Dravid. Then came MS Dhoni, Yuvraj Singh and Virat Kohli with the new millennium.

As mentioned time and again in the book, the great years over time have been 1949–50, 1952–55, 1959–60, 1963–66, 1969–75, 1981–82, 1986–88, 1990, 1992–94 and so on. While some of the outstanding cricketers were born in India, others were obviously born in different countries. Also, there was some kind of a patch of greatness associated with certain teams/countries. So, while some of the champion cricketers born in the 1950s belonged to India and the West Indies, others were born in the 1960s in Sri Lanka and Australia, which resulted in all these nations winning the World Cups one by one. The 1970s saw India and Australia sharing them, with a few of them sprinkled over in England too. The 1980s were once again great years for India and Australia. In the 1990s the focus seemed to shift to England. The later part of the 1990s also has some distinguished cricketers born in India, Sri Lanka and Australia.

Now, let's zoom in upon the lot born in the 1990s, since they are the hope for the future. Looking at the 1990s, the major years have been 1990, 1992, 1993, 1994 and 1997.

The last—1997—was an extraordinary year, when Pluto was in its own house and Planet-X came into its deepest exaltation in its nascent phase. This extremely potent circumstance would produce some of the greatest superstars in sports as well as other fields.

The 1997-born Malala Yousafzai is the youngest recipient of the Nobel Prize; Naomi Osaka is creating ripples in the tennis circuit; and Kylie Jenner is the new-age celebrity. Even in cricket some of the greatest players would be born in the same year, interestingly, in the last quarter.

Rishabh Pant has already made it big and is destined for greatness. Some of the others making waves in the IPL, like Khaleel Ahmed, Rinku Singh, Sarfaraz Khan and Mayank Markande were all born in the last quarter of 1997 and have possibilities of passing several milestones in their career. All of them have chances to play for the country successfully.

The next lot of cricketers with exciting horoscopes was born in the period 1998–2001. These players have the power of Pluto and Planet-X in their favour, but with a slightly lower impact. These players may play for the country, but their success, impact, scale and grandeur will be less than of those born in 1997. So players like Prithvi Shaw, Shubman Gill, Washington Sundar, Ishan Kishan, Shivam Mavi, Arjun Tendulkar and Kamlesh Nagarkoti could find relatively smaller amount of success compared to a Rishabh Pant or a Khaleel Ahmed. While Rishabh Pant would go on to be a cricket great, Prithvi Shaw would probably be very good but still short of great. Mind you, the 1998–2001 patch is no slouch; it is just that 1997 is a notch better.

The years 2002 and 2003 would produce some exceptional cricketers who will overtake the 1998–2001 patch cricketers. One such player visible now over the horizon is Prayas Ray Burman, who has just been selected for Royal Challengers Bangalore. There would be many more players born in 2002–03 who will be visible during the next two years and all of them will do better than the players from the previous patch.

But the greatest years of the century range from 2004 to 2006. These were the years when the high-impact planets, Uranus and Pluto, were in their own houses and Planet-X was in the deepest exaltation. Right now I can see one player who could go on to be a cricket legend from this patch: Samit Dravid.

There is definitely an Indian captain born in the year 2005. These boys will debut for India after 2021, when Pluto enters into exaltation once again, and they will be the greatest. The future Tendulkars, Pontings, Kapil Devs, Warners and Kohlis. While this chapter is being written in 2019, these boys must be around 13–15 years old, but they will shape the world of cricket in the future.

The talent scouts need to thoroughly examine and unearth their potential. Some of the greatest legends of the game were born then. Let us hope that the majority of them were born in India.

Prediction #49

What Will Happen to the Administration of the BCCI?

The BCCI has received a lot of flak during the recent months for its slow response and inefficiency in the handling of various matters and events. On 14th July 2015, the Supreme Court committee, headed by RM Lodha, suspended the owners of Rajasthan Royals and Chennai Super Kings from the Indian Premier League cricket tournament for a period of two years for their alleged involvement in betting. Later, in 2016, the panel headed by Justice Lodha also made many recommendations that could turn the BCCI transparent and accountable.

On 30th January 2017, on the recommendations of the Lodha committee, the Supreme Court appointed a four-member panel to run the day-to-day affairs of the BCCI[1]. The panel consisted of Ramachandra Guha—the historian and cricket writer; Diana Edulji—the former Indian women's cricket captain; Vinod Rai—the former Comptroller and Auditor General of India; and Vikram Limaye—CEO and MD of IDFC. Afterwards, Guha

---

1 PTI. (2017, January 30). *Supreme court appoints four-member panel to run BCCI.* Retrieved from: http://www.newindianexpress.com. Accessed on 17 February 2019.

resigned citing personal reasons and Limaye left due to his appointment as the new CEO and MD of the National Stock Exchange (NSE).

The four-member team became a two-member one and, for some time now, the two remaining admins have not agreed on or seen eye to eye on many matters. They have been quite sluggish in solving even mundane affairs and have become a laughing stock in public. The way the admin team handled the KL Rahul and Hardik Pandya *Koffee with Karan* chat show controversy became the butt of all jokes. Therefore, Sourav Ganguly and N Srinivasan have requested the Supreme Court to dissolve this panel and conduct fresh elections so that the BCCI can be fully functional once again.

So who will take over the BCCI after this temporary panel has been quashed?

The BCCI strongman, N Srinivasan, has an extraordinary horoscope that made him one of the biggest businessmen from south India. He turned a failing family business around and made it into a huge conglomerate, India Cements. Srinivasan's company has major stakes in Chennai Super Kings and the TNPL, to name a few. Unfortunately for Srinivasan, he is undergoing a very tough transit right now. The weakest planets in his horoscope are Uranus, Neptune and Pluto and all of them will work against his interests one by one. In any case he cannot make a comeback as the president now since he is over 70 and, according to the new recommendations, he doesn't qualify to contest. With Neptune and Pluto becoming powerful from 2021, he will slowly lose the stranglehold that he had on the BCCI.

After Sharad Pawar—the 1940-born, N Srinivasan—the 1945 born—became the BCCI chief. He was succeeded by Shashank Manohar, who was born in 1957. Manohar has the Pluto-and-Neptune power with him. So, there is a definite possibility of him landing a role in the corridors of the BCCI, since he has a clear advantage over N Srinivasan.

Does that mean it's going to be Shashank Manohar once again?

Not necessarily. There is a distinct possibility that neither of these two strong men will have a control over the BCCI in the future. Both of them have great horoscopes and both of them have had their great runs. The 1940-1945-1952 patch has had its glorious share of authority and control and now it's over. After the Supreme Court became involved in the clean-up, following the logical progression of events, there is a clear possibility that a person born in the 1960s or the 70s will be the new head honcho of the BCCI. Quite possible. So, watch out, it is going to get interesting over there.

Prediction #50

Will Lalit Modi Make a Comeback?

This man has a very interesting horoscope and he has lived up to it with an interesting life so far. With his devil-may-care attitude, brashness, arrogance and ruthless ambition, he created one of the greatest brands and success stories in world sports. But the same traits also ensured that he had a huge list of adversaries. Many of them wanted to see his back, and that may have resulted in his steepest and one of the fastest falls from grace.

Lalit Modi has always done things the way he has wanted to since his college days, when he pleaded guilty for the possession of cocaine, or married his mother's friend who was ten years his senior. His abrasive and confrontational approach shows the essence of the typical Aries-Scorpio in him. His third lord of the mind, Neptune, exalted in the tenth house (of career) resulted in his masterminding the biggest cash cow for the BCCI—the IPL.

The interesting story of his life is centred on the presence of an exalted Pluto in the eighth house (of adversities). Pluto ensured first that he had steep growth before pushing him off the pedestal. He is now at the epicentre of huge controversies, where he has taken powerful people like Srinivasan, Shashi Tharoor and others head on. Meanwhile, he was expelled from the BCCI on charges of bid rigging, accepting kickbacks and money laundering. He is currently in exile in London, while the Enforcement Directorate has launched a moneylaundering investigation against him and a few other BCCI officials. Modi has brushed it off saying that it is a political vendetta against him.

The eighth house indicates controversies, underworld dealings, bankruptcies, scams, litigations, illegal activities, scandals, disgrace and enemies. Modi has seen all of these. He refused to return to India, saying that there was a threat to his life and Mumbai Police endorsed this claim. Apparently, a well-known underworld don and his associate had sent hitmen to kill Modi and his family when the Modis were on a vacation in Thailand.

Modi's horoscope is an excellent illustration of what the lord of the underworld, Pluto, can do to you, especially when you have it exalted in your eighth house.

Interestingly, the same planetary position is also an indicator of transformation and great comebacks. That is a ray of hope for Modi. There really is a possibility of his making a comeback. Yes, it won't be easy because he still has Uranus in a weaker position, which would mean a huge backlash at home because Uranus lies in his fourth house (of home). It will not be easy for him.

Immediately after he launched the IPL in 2007, and it became a success story, Pluto entered into his twelfth house (of losses and foreign country). Hence, he had to live in a foreign land as a fugitive. But, with Pluto coming back into his first house (of personality) in 2021, he could come back into his own. His personality will be enhanced. He could expect some kind of respite from his problems and some factors responsible for maligning his name may get cleared. Don't be surprised if he gets a clean chit in some of the numerous cases against him. He may not be completely exonerated, but he could get some of his stripes back.

Also, Neptune will be transiting Modi's third house from 2022. Hence, he may come up with an interesting new venture once again, which should be unique and fantastic and probably even successful. So, yes, you haven't heard the last of Lalit Modi yet.

Astrological Tips for IPL Owners

28th January 2018.

When I expressed my unhappiness over the list of players an IPL team ended with, the part-owner said this to me:

'I tried everything. Also, at the auction table, things happen so fast that even before you realise it the player you always wanted has already shifted hands. Also understand that I, alone, cannot claim the player I want. The coach and the other owners also have a say in that.'

I understood the dilemma. I was annoyed since I had this opportunity to create a perfect 'astrologically balanced' team, which could go on to win the IPL, but the team fell considerably short of the required players. Cricketing logic overrules astro-logic many a time and it is perfectly understandable. The team did reasonably well, much better than they had done in the previous years, but I knew it was a missed opportunity.

I gave this team some secret tips. Now, I'm listing them in the open. You can use them to build a successful IPL team. If they are implemented, you can be sure that the stars are with you and hence you are destined for success. Whatever is meant to happen will happen anyway, but you can always try and put in your best.

Some teams have changed their names without realising that it is not just the name of the team that matters, but also *when* it is named. And not to mention, who the captain is.

Remember that the captain is the most important component in the entire process. Appoint one who has a great potential, but hasn't won any major event as a captain before.

A captain born in the years 1986, 1987, 1990, 1993, 1994 has better chances of winning the upcoming tournaments than the others. Of course, individual horoscopes do matter. Look into those too. In case there are a couple of captains with the same year of birth, then the person with the better individual horoscope should be chosen.

1. Pack in a group of players who, too, have potential, but haven't been part of or won major tournaments. This could include players born in the years just mentioned, if you are convinced they are really good but haven't had a chance with better teams before.
2. Hire a coach, who is very good (but not pedigree) and doesn't have a great history of successes. Watch out for coaches born in 1965–76, 1980–82. These are the golden years. One obviously needs to look into other considerations regarding individual horoscopes.
3. Ensure that there aren't any veterans in the team. Do not include players who are way younger or way older than the current generation.
4. Avoid appointing a captain either too old or too young compared to other captains in the tournament. If, say, the average age of the captains is 33, don't have a captain who is 38 or 25.
5. If you have already won a tournament with a team, don't be too emotional and keep the core of the team with you. Release some players who have achieved peak success with you. You cannot extract more than what is destined.

Afterword

When I started pursuing astrology, my biggest desire and hope was to change people's lives. The mystery surrounding the subject and the abstruse logic and practices with which it was associated made me think that here was the key to bring happiness into people's lives. I hoped to use astrology as a magic wand that could substantially alter lives.

How wrong I was! It took me some time to realise that whatever is meant to happen, will. After almost 25 years of being an astrologer, I can say that I cannot alter anything. No one can. If anyone claims that they can change people's lives, well, you need to think twice. They are claiming to be gods. Yes, I can bring in clarity about the eventuality. Astrology is a tool that helps you know exactly what will happen—good or bad—and be prepared for it. If it is good, you can maximise the joy. If it is not, then you learn how to handle it. You do get a chance to look at the best possible ways of dealing with a calamity and put up your best foot forward even if you have that smallest chance.

Incident 1:

A popular producer of TV serials called me for a 'sure-shot success' movie project. She told me to look into the horoscopes of some filmstars and come up with a combination that would make a successful film. I came up with some combinations, using the birth details of many actors and also gave her some alternatives in case some of them weren't available. The producer's team tried hard, but couldn't get all of those actors and the director together on board. While some of them were busy, some were not affordable and, well, the project was shelved.

Incident 2:

Another film director gave me a list of the birth details of some young, unknown actors and sought help in deciding the lead hero and the heroine for a film. He couldn't go with the top pair I suggested as the actress was not in the good books of the producer and the actor, according to him, didn't have the 'spark'. They went ahead with a pair I asked them to avoid. The movie sank without a trace.

Incident 3:

When this popular yesteryear south Indian heroine asked me to look into her horoscope, what struck me the most was her strong eighth house. Her question was pertaining to her spiritual growth. While her ninth house did look promising, and I told her that she would definitely go down the spiritual path, she nonetheless needed to be careful as her name could be drawn into some unnecessary controversies. After a few months, when she told me about her being enchanted by the teachings of a particular young spiritual guru, I warned her about the signs in her chart that spelt dangers ahead. She was happier that she had finally found her source of happiness and probably ignored my warnings. She became the epicentre of a sex scandal that shook the entire south India.

Incident 4:

A yesteryear north Indian heroine, who had acted in some of the biggest hits in Hindi cinema and was also very famous down south, showed me the horoscope of her son who wanted to emulate his mother. I warned her that he would never make it in the movies and suggested an alternative profession where he would be successful. The mother, however, had no choice but to bow down to the wish of the son. Depleting her life's savings, she paid a fortune to the producer who gave her son a break as a hero, but he didn't make any impact and the movie didn't even run for a week.

Incident 5:

When my sister Salate was pregnant, she asked me about the best '*muhurat*' when she could deliver a 'super' child who would be successful, healthy and happy. As the time limit given by the doctor was about two weeks, I could come up with a handful of good *muhurats* when she could deliver such a child. A couple of days before the date, Salate went into labour and had to be operated. Brushing aside all our plans, the baby girl arrived when *she* planned to.

When you look at all these cases objectively, you realise that all the events were meant to happen. I couldn't prevent any of them from happening despite my best intentions. The TV serial producer and the film director were going through one of the toughest phases in their careers, astrologically, and so couldn't put together successful projects. The south Indian heroine always had this calamity looming large in her life, while the north Indian heroine was destined to lose most of her savings to her loved one. My sister's daughter came with her own destiny and I wasn't supposed to mess around with that.

Now I'm to going to tell you exactly how astrology *can* help someone. As this book is on cricket, out of hundreds of case studies, let me focus on this one which has a background of cricket.

Incident 6:

Raghunath Reddy (name changed) must have easily been over six feet tall. When he looked down to shake my hands, I could sense the uneasy discomfort uncharacteristic in a man with his tall frame, strong hands and broad shoulders. He looked almost apologetic about being there.

His horoscope was extraordinary. The magical planet, Neptune, was very strongly placed in the third house of the hands. But there were multitudes of weak planets in the chart in the eighth, sixth and the first houses, indicating huge challenges in his career and growth as a person. There were indications regarding his inability to fight competition and his career being derailed due to some strange, inexplicable situations, conspiracies or unfortunate cirumstances. There were enough pointers to show that the magic of Neptune wouldn't materialise at all in his life and it would remain a case of 'what if…'.

His story was unbelievable. When he was 11, he had already played for his state in the Under-13 team. He was one of the promising fast bowlers in India when he was 14. He could consistently bowl at about 100 mph, something considered extraordinary for a boy of that age. He often rattled the stumps of the upcoming batsmen and was feared by many. He even attended the camps conducted by the BCCI. A talent scout of an IPL team, too, approached his father and took his details.

His coach, who had spotted him on the street throwing balls superfast, had offered his services for free and Raghunath considered him as his god. The son of a rickshaw driver dreamt of a great future ahead.

When Raghunath was about 16, his coach met him the evening before he was to play an extremely important match. He told him to bowl a little faster than he usually did. 'See, people have started noticing you. You will come on the radar only if you clock a higher mph consistently. Target 120 mph now. Just throw the ball as hard as you can.' Raghunath just went all out in that match. After he had put in all his energy into his bowling, the coach would signal to him to bowl the next ball even harder. Raghunath was ready to lay down his life for the man who had given some hope in life. He flung the next ball as fast as he could. Then the most shocking thing happened. The umpire warned him for 'chucking'. A stunned Raghunath looked at his coach. The unperturbed coach signalled to him to repeat the action without bothering about the umpire. After the next ball, the umpire called him out for chucking again and, after a few more balls, he was taken off bowling by his captain.

By the end of the match day, Raghunath noticed a curious exchange between the coach and the umpire. Raghunath didn't know if it was his imagination or if he really saw his coach wink at the umpire. The local newspapers carried stories of him being a cheat and a chucker. In the next match, another upcoming fast bowler, Vikram Rao (name changed), the son of a local MP, played in place of him.

Raghunath's chances of ever making it as a cricketer became less and less and his performances started slackening. Whenever he got a chance, he was confused about how he should bowl. Should be bowl at his best speed or try to better it? He ended up giving away too many runs and a period of inconsistency started with his confidence hitting a new low. Slowly, he was overlooked in state cricket and fell off the radar of the selectors. Raghunath learnt that Vikram, too, hadn't gone too far in his career and had enrolled in a college in London instead. Disillusioned, Raghunath quit playing cricket, the biggest dream of his life, just at the age of 18.

I told the tired and defeated Raghunath that all was not lost in his life. He was never destined to be a cricketer in the first place. It could remain a passion, but it was not meant to be his calling. His Neptune was only a mirage. It was there, yet not there. It was a result of his past-life karmas. He was supposed to undergo this huge disappointment in his life, which would rankle him forever. The incident was meant to happen. An incident which had come with a lot of lessons.

His real success would come from the fourth and the ninth houses. The fourth house indicates food, land, properties, etc. and the ninth house is about being a subject matter expert, a consultant, coach, guru and also indicates education. Post our meeting, Raghunath successfully set up a restaurant business and also doubled up as an education consultant.

He is now in alignment with his karma and knows what he was destined to be. In fact, now he feels that education is another field where his passion lies and he also finds food a fascinating business. He even takes out time to keep himself healthy, playing cricket with his business partners during weekends, and also mentors some street kids in fast bowling. He no longer feels sad that he couldn't be a cricketer who played for India. He has accepted that he will never be another Kapil Dev. But he is trying to be the best at what he can be—being Raghunath for his family. And, most importantly, for himself.

What started out of curiosity as an interesting way to kill time turned out to be a passion of a lifetime for me. The original intention to discover my calling has materialised and now it is all about deciphering, decoding and translating the mysteries of a particular planetary alignment, be it for a person, an event or for an organisation.

The planets and stars that twinkle in the sky have all the mysteries of life within them. They show us how exactly our lives will unfold. The planetary alignments at the time of our birth indicate the past life karmas and hence the current life learnings and possibilities. What is intriguing is that everything can be predicted, after a lot of effort and research. Anything and everything! Because of just one reason. As above, so below.

Acknowledgements

The websites *astrodatabank.com* and *astrotheme.com* were very important sources where I found the most accurate birth details of sports persons, which helped a lot in my research.

A big thank you to all Indian cricketers and their parents, who offered me the accurate birth details when I approached them. It helped me predict many events like India's winning the World Cup, the IPLs, etc.

Thank you, Derek, Rutvick Mehta, Tauz Rizvi and the team at *DNA*, for connecting me with many sports stars or helping me collect and collate their birth details, including those of Sachin Tendulkar, through various sources.

Thank you very much, Divya Dubey, for helping me with the initial editing of the manuscript, and going beyond the ambit of your job to make the entire process simpler for me. The questions you posed helped me shape the book to its current form. Your inputs at every juncture helped me gain a better understanding of the reader's perspective. Thank you, also, for introducing me to Dipankar Mukherjee.

Thank you, Indrani Ganguly, for the quick and neat final edits. Thank you, Sourish Mitra, for the thoughtful cover.

Lastly, but most importantly, thank you, Dipankar Mukherjee, for your guts and for putting your trust in an 'unknown quantity'. Many publishers refused to take up the book for the fear of the predictions failing and the backlash they might have to face. The final draft took a beautiful and interesting turn because of your timely intervention and valuable suggestions. Special thanks to you!

GREENSTONE LOBO
April, 2019

About the Author

Greenstone Lobo read his own birth chart at the age of 16 and has been fascinated by this science ever since. At the time of his graduation in Chemistry, his notebooks were filled with more horoscopes than chemical formulae. Now, as a Human Resources professional, he has also researched, tested and practised the principles of astrology in the corporate environment for over 22 years.

After extensive research on the Indian and Western astrology systems, both of which he found incomplete, Greenstone delved deeper into astronomy as well as astrology. He has the distinction of being the only astrologer on the planet to have discovered the relevance and influence of planetoids X (NASA: 2007 RH283), Y (NASA: 1999 JV127) and Z (NASA: 2008 FC76) upon human destiny. Based on it, he has devised his own system for reading birth charts and making predictions, which has produced excellent results so far. Amongst several other predictions, Greenstone correctly prophesied in 2011, against popular belief, that India would win the ICC World Cup; and in 2015, he proclaimed Australia as the winner.

Greenstone conducts regular workshops for aspiring astrologers in different parts of India. He is the author of the book, *What is Your True Zodiac Sign?* (Celestial Books). He has been writing a regular column on sports astrology, 'Octozone', in the popular Indian daily, *DNA*, since 2008. He has also been a columnist for *Anandabazar Patrika* and *Sportskeeda.com*. His opinions, advisory columns, predictions and articles have been published in the *Times of India*, *Mumbai Mirror*, *The Telegraph*, *Life Positive* and *Sangbad Pratidin*. Besides this he has appeared on RadioCity, Radio One, Radio Mirchi and KCOR (USA).

Follow the Author:

Website: http://www.greenstonelobo.com/about-greenstone.html

Facebook: https://www.facebook.com/ScientificAstrologer/

Twitter: @GreenstoneLobo

For past predictions of Greenstone Lobo:

http://www.greenstonelobo.com/popular-predictions.html

Generate your FREE horoscope here:

http://www.truezodiacsign.com/calculator.html

The calculator was originally incorporated to help those who wanted to know their 'true' zodiac sign. But now the horoscope in its entirety with all the 16 bodies can be seen in the chart. Have fun knowing the planetary positions of all those who matter to you.